MW00610212

Lonely 🌐 planet

HIDDEN LIBRARIES

THE WORLD'S MOST UNUSUAL BOOK DEPOSITORIES

DC HELMUTH

Foreword by **NANCY PEARL**

CONTENTS

FOREWORD

One truth I've learned in my long career as a librarian is that a library serves different purposes for different people. I've seen how a library can bring a community together, how it can help users find the information they need to live better lives, whether it's a book discussion group or information about who to talk to about your electricity bill.

Librarians in public libraries can share the joy of reading a good book and assist people looking for their next great read. Research libraries delve deep into their subject matter, serving both specialists in their professional work and the interested layperson. Archival libraries store rare works, manuscripts, or the personal papers of a significant figure. An archival library can be like an art museum, insofar that it's not just the words it 'contains' that are of interest, but the materials themselves. Special conditions (temperature, humidity, level of light, the use of gloves) are maintained to protect its delicate contents. Every library is valuable in its particular way, and each is an example of the role and importance of libraries in the community of humanity.

Although I've spoken at libraries in many countries, I never imagined, until I read Diana Helmuth's fascinating and informative guide to 'hidden' libraries all over the world, that, to paraphrase Hamlet, there are actually more libraries, and kinds of libraries, than are dreamt of in our library science classes. A 'hidden' library, then, is a library that likely would be unfamiliar to most of us, no matter how much we describe ourselves as readers and lovers of libraries.

When I read Helmuth's book, there was only one library that I was even tangentially familiar with: the Haskell Free Library and Opera House, which straddles the US-Canadian border. The others she describes were a revelation and a delightful surprise.

And all of them began as someone or some group's recognition of a certain need in their community. I was of course familiar with bookmobiles, a staple of many libraries. In fact, my first job as a librarian was working on a bookmobile; we took books to housing projects and underserved communities all over Detroit. In Helmuth's research she discovered the Biblioburro in the Magdalena Valley, near Colombia's Caribbean coast. Starting with one burro, it now employs over 20 traveling donkey libraries. Then there's the Horse Library in Hawassa, Ethiopia, which is not, as might be thought, a collection of books about horses, but rather a collection of books delivered to outlying communities by horse.

In Garissa, Kenya, camels delivered books to the desert nomads: "Every morning the Kenyan Library Service prepared three camels for travel. The party consisted of a librarian in charge, two assistants and a skilled camel herdsman who knew how to keep the moody beasts healthy and in check. One camel was tasked with carrying a whopping 400 books. Another was packed with a tent, reading mat and chairs. The third just waited for one of the other two to fall apart so it could sub in. These librarians and animals regularly worked until nightfall, ranging 7 miles (11km) in any direction from their home base, Monday through Thursday."

I loved finding out about St Catherine's Monastery Library, in Sinai, Egypt, in which the oldest texts date back to the 4th century. I learned there's a library in London that is all about journalists and journalism: the St Bride Foundation Library, which can be found, where else, on Fleet Street. There are vending machine libraries in Shenzhen, China, and an open-air library in Magdeburg, Germany.

There are actually 13 different libraries in Chinguetti, Mauritania, deep in the Saharan desert. The village was founded in 777 CE as a trading post. "Chinguetti's Rue des Savants (street of intelligent ones) gained fame as a gathering place for students, Imams and pilgrims on their way to and from Mecca to debate the finer points of Islamic law. Sometimes, these sages left books behind." These libraries

– many of which are run by the families who own these precious materials – now contain over 6,000 texts, some from the 9th century.

I knew about the tragic destruction of the great library in Alexandria, Egypt, in the 3rd century, of course, but Helmuth discovered numerous other no-longer-in-existence hidden libraries. I was most interested in the Lost Library of the Moscow Tsars, which, as Helmuth points out, might not ever have existed at all. The Golden Library, as it was known, has never been found, and the treasures it contained (if indeed the library existed) are beyond measure.

I'm going to stop now, partly because I want you to stop reading this foreword and begin *Hidden Libraries* to unearth its joys yourself, but mostly because I'm going to call my travel agent and have her start planning my trip to visit the libraries herein.

– NANCY PEARL

THE PRISON LIBRARY PROJECT

CALIFORNIA, USA

HOW TO FIND IT

586 W 1st St, Claremont, CA. Located on the first floor of the historic Citrus Packing House in the Claremont Village.
+1 909 626 3066; claremontforum.org/ prisonlibraryproject

You can visit the Prison Library Project bookshop in person or donate specific books that prisoners have requested by visiting the Prison Library Project's wish list at bookshop.org.

Because they're located within buildings that are inaccessible to the general public, you could argue that every prison library in the world is a hidden library. Books that are inside a prison carry a different weight than books that are, as they say, 'on the outside'. Internet use inside prisons is extremely limited, and smartphones are typically banned. Books are not just charming pieces of decor but the primary source of entertainment, education and social connection that prisoners have with the world beyond the walls.

Because prisons have their own libraries, it might seem strange that non-profit organizations exist in the US to send books to prisoners; yet these library programmes are more in demand than ever. Sergio Perez is the project director of the Prison Library Project (PLP), a national non-profit that channels books from the outside world into prisons. "Within the last year, we've been getting a lot of calls from chaplains, correctional officers and wardens to help stock their libraries," he says. "Prisons aren't allocated a lot of money to purchase many books, and most are stocked with titles that are either very outdated or physically falling apart. So when they need help, they send their requests to us. In the past we used to reach out to them and ask what they needed. That was a very bureaucratic process. It took a week for someone to answer the phone. When the request comes from them, though, the inmates can get their books much faster.

OPPOSITE The Prison Library Project sources, sorts and delivers books to people behind bars. Their public bookstore helps raise funds for shipping fees.

© Tomas Yamaguchi

"Books are not just charming pieces of decor,
but the primary source of entertainment, education
and social connection that prisoners have with
the world beyond the walls."

We don't have as much overhead on our side. I'd say we get between 1000 and 2000 requests a month from state and federal prisoners."

The Prison Library Project has operated out of a physical shop in Claremont, California since 1986. In a college town where books are everywhere, the store serves as a fundraising base, book donation station and community centre. "We rent out space in the Bookshop for minimal costs, too," Perez explains. "We have artists doing gallery showings, we host writing group meetings, musicians come to give concerts. There's a weekly farmer's market too. All of it generates awareness of the cause and helps us bring in income for shipping the books and purchasing special request books."

Perez estimates that 80% of the Bookshop's titles are comprised of used books, donated by the community. The remaining 20% are brand new books that the PLP purchases. The number one request from inmates? "Dictionaries," says Perez. "And thesauruses. A lot of people think it might be the bible, but it's not. We also get a lot of requests for GED [General Education Development] study books and composition books. Then it's a lot of sci-fi and fantasy, law books and study courses for different vocations. We do get occasional requests for some inappropriate material (which we don't facilitate), but it's not that common. We try to match the request of the individual. And if we can't – for example, law books

go out of date very quick – we send them a resource list of other NPOs [non-profit organizations] that may help them."

"Some of these books are expensive, like a transgender study book or a CDL [commercial driver's license] study course book. We'll often fundraise in order to purchase those books new. And if we get it, we send the book to the prisoner."

A tricky problem faced by free library programmes like the PLP is the quality of the donations they receive. Well-meaning people drop off droves of books, many of which are out of date, falling apart or will never be requested by the inmates (children's books, for example). "Probably only 60% of books that get donated are viable, that's just the reality," reflects Perez. "We will try and pass on what we can to another NPO. And if the books have mold or water damage, we send them to other places that turn them into shoes or toilet paper. One place in Mexico turns old books into those spongy basketball court floors. We are 100% volunteer run, and it takes a lot of labor to sort through the donated books. But if we give donators too many parameters, it turns them off. If people give us books they've valued and enjoyed and they don't see we appreciate them, it turns them away from donating entirely. And we don't want that. We have enough volunteers and storage space to process the books. It can be daunting. But we make it work."

When Perez is asked about some of his more interesting stories, he replies "the thank you letters. Some of them are from lifers, or people who don't have families. Some don't have any money to buy books from the outside. Some of them are really trying to turn their lives around, take a course, but the prison doesn't have the textbook they need. When someone says in a letter, 'look, I made a mistake, but when I get out of here I want something to do, but I need help getting that education,' that moves me a lot."

OPPOSITE Stacks of books are ready to be packaged and shipped to the prisoners who requested them.

BELOW The Traveler beckons weary road trippers to take a rest with warm food and good books.

THE TRAVELER RESTAURANT

CONNECTICUT, USA

HOW TO FIND IT

1257 Buckley Hwy,
Union, CT
facebook.com/
thefoodandbookpeople

There is a proper
bookstore connected
to the restaurant,
selling the hottest
bestsellers and
bric-a-brac - just
in case the free
section doesn't
have what you're
looking for.

There are but a few rules in your average library: no talking, no running and, usually, no eating. The Traveler, a roadside diner just on the border of Massachusetts and Connecticut, challenges this norm. The restaurant boasts a sign in its suburban-looking front yard, loudly announcing 'Food and Books' to weary travellers crossing through the wide, open plains of Interstate 84.

The restaurant serves up American favourites like hamburgers, chicken noodle soup and hot fudge sundaes. But the books are the main pull – rows and rows of them. Step into the dining room and bookshelves are everywhere you look, flanking tables and crisscrossing back walls. The downstairs is a gigantic bookstore for used books, just in case the upstairs wasn't enough for you.

With each meal, customers are invited to take home three free books from the restaurant's main collection. The owners estimate they give away 1000 to 2000 books each week, many of which are donated by libraries in the region.

The Traveler's original owner, Marty Doyle, was a bibliophile who grew up during the Great Depression and with a mindset to never let a good book go. But by the 1980s, he found himself with a problem: he now had a personal library of thousands of books, beginning to overtake his home. So he moved a healthy portion of them into his restaurant and encouraged every person who entered to take one – even if they were only stopping to use the bathroom. Each book was considered an indefinite loan, until when (or if) the customer decided to return and trade it for another.

Doyle began receiving donations from librarians and rural neighbours – many of which, he realized, were rare and valuable. Hence, the creation of the bookstore.

BELOW Customers are surrounded by books during their meal, and reading at the table is encouraged. **OPPOSITE** Each diner is offered three books to take home.

Doyle hired a retired librarian and transformed the restaurant's cellar into a vault of rare and valuable tomes.

In the 1990s, Doyle sold his restaurant to Karen and Art Murdock, who saw no reason to fix a system that wasn't broken. Today, every customer who visits the diner is still allowed to take three free books home with them. The Murdocks estimate that since they took over, the restaurant has given away close to 100,000 books every year. They range from paper-backs, children's books, romance novels, cookbooks, histories and more.

"It takes a special establishment to understand that sometimes, the best part of visiting a family restaurant isn't the food but the distractions around you that prevent you from arguing with that family," wrote Ilana Gordon, who grew up near the restaurant, in *The Takeout* in 2020. "And that alone is a good enough reason to pull off the interstate and investigate."

BELOW The books stored in the cottonwood tree's Little Free Library are kept safe thanks to a well-fitted roof and a feline neighborhood watch committee.

LITTLE FREE LIBRARY IN A COTTONWOOD TREE

HOW TO FIND IT

*716 North A St,
Coeur d'Alene, ID*

This is
technically a
librarian's front
garden. We suggest
putting on your
best behaviour.

IDAHO, USA

If you live in the US, you may have seen 'Little Free Libraries' around your neighbourhood. The movement was founded in 2009 by Todd Bol in Wisconsin, to promote community literacy between people who had books to spare. Today there are over 75,000 Little Free Libraries in 88 countries across the world. Although the official name is trademarked, plenty of unofficial free libraries exist across the world.

Typically a Little Free Library resembles a large birdhouse or mailbox, sometimes hand painted or decorated with children's stickers and finger paints. You can order a prefab version from the non-profit itself or make your own. In Coeur d'Alene, Idaho, Sharalee Armitage Howard has done just that, turning the 110-year-old cottonwood tree in her front yard into a Little Free Library. The glowing, back-lit bookcase in the heart of a 10-ft (3-m) tree stump looks like something that belongs in Bilbo Baggins' world rather than our own.

Howard is a librarian with Coeur d'Alene Public Libraries and an artist-in-residence at various primary schools in the area. Her specialty is teaching children

© Christi Iffergan

the process of writing, illustrating and assembling books, many of which are sold at farmers' markets to raise money for humanitarian causes.

The library in the cottonwood tree is, technically, an upcycling project. Howard discovered the tree was dead when it dropped a branch on her son's car. However, she found herself irrevocably attached to the old Cottonwood, and after the top section was cut away, began to think of ways to repurpose the stump.

"Immediately I could envision the little steps going up to it," she told *Atlas Obscura* in 2019. "I knew I'd do a lot of features to make it match the house. You just have these 'what if' moments and then your brain starts figuring out how to make it work."

Howard scooped out the deceased insides of the tree stump, then created a box measured to fit inside the hole into which shelves and books were ultimately placed. Stone steps were placed at the foot of the tree, leading to a glass door – a repurposed vintage window painted a regal green – and the case decorated with a lining of fairy-sized books. A lantern sits above the door, installed thanks to the help of Howard's electrician neighbour. Finally, the stump is crowned with a slanted chalet roof, protecting the books and, one imagines, any perusing hobbits from the sun or rain.

She unveiled the creation on 10 December 2018, and it became an internet hit. "There's been a steady stream of cars," she said. "There's literally been people waiting for other people to take their turn."

BELOW The Stony Island Arts Bank
repurposed a crumbling financial building
into a thriving cultural library.

STONY ISLAND ARTS BANK

ILLINOIS, USA

HOW TO FIND IT

*6760 S Stony Island Ave, Chicago, IL
rebuild-foundation.org*

`The library is
open most of the
day, but often
hosts music,
theatre and dance
events in the
evening. Check
their website
for the latest
calendar.`

If you walk down Stony Island Avenue in Chicago's South Side, you'll come across the old facade of Stony Island Savings and Loan – an imposing neoclassical relic from 1923. In the 1980s, the bank was shut down and remained vacant for decades, crumbling and forgotten. The roof collapsed, giving a home to years of snow, rain and sun. A wrecking ball seemed the only merciful fate for the place.

Then in 2013, Theaster Gates, a professor at the University of Chicago and award-winning visual artist and urban planner, bought the 1860 sq-metre (20,000 sq-ft) building from the city for $1. It was just days before its scheduled demolition. His dream: to turn the decrepit money bank into a thriving 'arts bank'.

In a 2015 press release, Gates describes the project as "an institution of and for the South Side," "a repository for African American culture and history," and "a space for neighborhood residents to preserve, access, reimagine and share their heritage, as well as a destination for artists, scholars, curators and collectors to research and engage with South Side history."

Today the Stony Island Arts Bank is a reading library, a gallery, artist residence, media archive and home for the Rebuild Foundation, a non-profit organization founded by Gates that fosters culture and development in underinvested Chicago neighbourhoods. Above all, it's an active community centre and laboratory for Black art and artists.

The building has been artfully restored with several details of the bank's history preserved, including peeling paint and damaged ceiling tiles, to merge the sense of past and present.

The library contains thousands of books, set up in stunning wall-to-wall bookcases in the former bank rooms. Beyond the written word, the library contains treasures such as the vinyl collection of House music legend Frankie Knuckles (with signed records from the likes of Grace Jones and Whitney Houston). Additionally, there is a historic collection of periodicals and books donated by John H. Johnson, founder of *Ebony* and *Jet* magazines (including a first edition of *The Best of Simple* with a personal note to Johnson from author Langston Hughes himself). A vintage card catalogue houses 60,000 glass photographic slides from the University of Chicago, illustrating history from the Palaeolithic era to the 20th century. Finally, the library houses an Edward J. Williams Collection of 4000 objects of so-called 'negrobilia' – historical pop-culture artefacts that feature stereotypical images of Black people.

"Projects like this require belief more than they require funding," Gates told *Fast Company* in 2015. "If there's not a kind of belief, motivation and critical aggregation of people who believe with you in a project like this, it cannot happen. The city is starting to realize that there might be other ways of imagining upside beside 'return on investment' and financial gain."

BELOW Few images exist of 'Fort Patti', the
OWS library's short-lived, official home base.
It was open 24 hours a day and staffed by
professional volunteer librarians.

THE PEOPLE'S LIBRARY OF OCCUPY WALL STREET

In Memoriam

NEW YORK, USA

On 17 September 2011 protestors swarmed Wall Street, demanding an end to corporate greed, economic inequality and the influence of money in politics. The Occupy Wall Street (OWS) protest was a reaction to the condensation of power amongst the nation's 1% richest people, and it did as its name suggested: physically occupied the biggest financial centre in the US for two solid months.

Within the makeshift encampments that OWS protesters created, formal leadership was eschewed in favour of group consensus. In many ways, OWS was a kind of socialist experiment, a camp that sought to prove the functionality of direct democracy in the face of the hierarchical leadership it was fighting against. Of course, it had a library.

Betsy Fagin, inspired by a New York University library science student who dropped off a box of books to the camp, brought the idea of an official library to the General Assembly. Residents, corporations and authors began to contribute books. Musician Patti Smith donated a tent in which to store the growing treasure trove, nicknamed 'Fort Patti'. The newborn library contained political texts from across the spectrum: holy scriptures from multiple faiths, children's books and all manner of fiction. It offered weekly poetry readings on Friday nights, provided a reference service that was frequently staffed by professional librarians, who could connect a visitor to an outside library, if Fort Patti did not have what they needed. LibraryThing – an online library catalogue system – donated a free lifetime membership to the project. The library also contained a lighted reading room, public laptop computers and free Wi-Fi.

For most donation-only libraries, donated books are a mixed blessing. Many cannot be used because of poor condition or incorrect audience and it takes hours of effort to sort through the lot. This is why many donation-dependent libraries are picky about what they accept and keep. In a departure from this trend, books donated to The People's Library were never rejected, even if they seemed at odds with the ideology behind the protest. Zachary Loeb, one of Fort Patti's volunteer librarians, said the library's collection policy had two points: "everything we have was donated to us, and we accept everything." He later reflected that because of this, "not only was the Library for the people but, as they are responsible for its creation, that it is of the people." Filmmaker Udi Aloni would go on to tell *Al Jazeera*, "the library was great because people gave more than they took. OWS was not just a place for activism but also a place for education and rethinking; not for just blathering on when you don't know, but being humble and willing to learn."

The library was under threat almost as soon as it was brought into existence. On 13 October 2011, Brookfield Properties, the owner of Zuccotti Park – the site of the occupy camp – notified the protestors that a 'cleaning' was imminent. Overnight, approximately 2000 books were taken out of Fort Patti for protection, only for Brookfield Properties to concede to public pressure and cancel. The books were brought back to Fort Patti. But another threat was around the corner.

In the predawn hours of 15 November 2011, New York's Police and Sanitation Departments came to shut OWS down. The encampments were disassembled and all their pieces loaded onto rubbish trucks. The mayor of New York at that time, Michael Bloomberg, claimed the library's books were not thrown away, but when OWS librarians came to collect them they would only find 902 volumes. The Fort Patti tent, laptops, and stamps used to identify library resources were missing, along with thousands of books, including signed copies donated by renowned authors and irreplaceable historical documents from the camp itself.

The American Library Association called Bloomberg's actions 'unacceptable', because libraries "serve as the cornerstone of our democracy and must be safeguarded." They went on to say that the "very existence of the People's Library demonstrates that libraries are an organic part of all communities." UC Irvine history professor Mark LeVine said that "tents can be replaced, even most personal effects.

But destroying books is like destroying the soul of the movement."

The OWS librarians, represented by Norman Siegel, sued the city, mayor Michael Bloomberg, police commissioner Raymond Kelly, and sanitation commissioner John Doherty in federal court. They won and were awarded $366,700 in damages.

Although Fort Patti lives no more, like the OWS movement, the People's Library still lives on. A few mobile carts still make their rounds in Liberty Plaza. You can reach out to the OWS librarians and see the full catalogue at peopleslibrary.wordpress.com.

LEFT Protesters took over Wall Street for 59 days, demanding an end to corporate greed. **BELOW** Fort Patti may be a memory, but the OWS library still lives online.

BELOW The KIDS Corner Library waited
patiently for patrons. A secret code was
required to access the collection.

KIDS CORNER LIBRARY

In Memoriam

NEW YORK, USA

Colin McMullan was a man obsessed. It was 2007, and he wanted to build libraries everywhere, both for kids and for KIDS – the members of the Kindness and Imagination Development Society – a group for "people committed to (re)developing their childhood selves".

"I had this great angle on it, using a loophole in public space regulation that allows the proliferation of newsracks everywhere," McMullan reflects on his personal website. "Why not a non-corporate version in the form of little public libraries? I mean I was writing grants, making models, planning budgets, talking to city agencies, recruiting librarians. I thought maybe I was going to create a non-profit organization or something and spend my life building miniature libraries all over the world. I got pretty worked up about it, I really did."

McMullan is an artist, with a focus on public interactions that compel their viewers to question the concepts of borders and property. For his first library, he crafted a small chamber about the size of a kennel, lining it with weatherproof custom-made boards, two windows, and a steeple roof. A pint-sized red door announced its mission to passers-by: "Welcome! This library is meant to encourage us all to publish and share information about local resources, issues, events, the many personal matters we care about deeply." The finished product was so tiny, it has been a frequent contender for the title of World's Smallest Library.

This was just the first. McMullan began setting up various guerrilla libraries across New York City. Some were installed within the bruised insides of old

BELOW Official library cards imbued young patrons responsibility of helping care for the pint-sized library. OPPOSITE The library was a treasured sight in New York's Bushwick neighborhood.

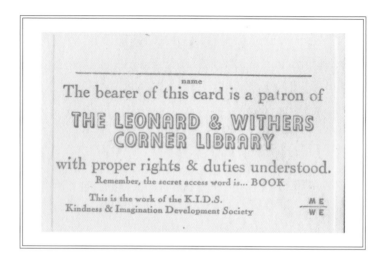

public telephone boxes (which the telephone companies invariably came by to uproot), others from old writing desks (one of which was set ablaze by, one can only assume, a bibliophobic arsonist). It seemed protections for these little libraries were necessary.

McMullan's original library with the orange door was thusly cladded with wheels, locked to a signpost, and, in a radical departure from almost every other free neighbourhood library, padlocked. "If you wanted to use it you just had to know the combo (B-O-O-K)," writes McMullan. "That worked really well, people respected the contents much more than when it was wide open."

The lock was not the only thing that differentiates the KIDS Corner Library from its other free library peers. The organizing group (KIDS) began to issue library cards to neighbourhood children, announcing them members of 'The Leonard & Withers Corner Library, with proper rights and duties understood.' The anachronistic cards were letterpress printed by McMullan and contain a section for the child's name, as well as space to write down the secret access

code, just in case the child's memory needed some assistance. The library operated on an honesty system, but with some extra flourish. Every object inside had its own catalogue card, on which the borrower was instructed to write down their name and the date borrowed. The card was then left in the 'catalogue' box in the back of the library, and the item was due back two weeks later.

Gabriela Alva joined McMullan as co-librarian early in the project, eventually building a website for the library which reflected its current on-the-ground offerings. McMullan's work eventually took him to Connecticut, but the corner library remained, sturdy and stocked, under the care of Alva.

McMullan's library went by many names: The KIDS Corner Library, the Leonard and Withers Library, the World's Smallest Library or simply the little box at the corner of Bogart and Harrison Place in Bushwick. It was stocked with children's books, zines, graphic novels, CDs, DVDs, maps, leaflets and other curiosities, and was proudly free for the enjoyment of all – all you had to do was know the password.

BELOW The Street Books library team has been circulating books in Portland since 2011. **OPPOSITE** The famous cart acts as stacks, donation desk and return basket – all on wheels.

STREET BOOKS

OREGON, USA

HOW TO FIND IT

The library makes several regular stops around Portland so patrons can easily find it. The updated list of locations is at: streetbooks.org/hours streetbooks.org.

The library offers books and also reading glasses, should patrons need them. You can follow them on Instagram @street. books.

Hidden libraries often have a way of serving people that the rest of society also considered hidden. This is especially true in the case of the Street Books bicycle library, in Portland.

Portland is a proud literary city. Multnomah County Library is often considered the busiest in the nation, when you compare circulation numbers against population size. However, public libraries – while constantly seeking to make themselves accessible to every citizen – still have a few requirements for joining. They typically include a photo ID, and the ability to pay back overdue book fines.

Laura Moulton, Portland resident, writer and professor, understood these requirements are considered modest to most people, but are in fact prohibitive to many. So, she created a library designed to serve Portland's people who do not have a photo ID, or the means to pay book fees – the people who live under overpasses, in tents, and in doorways; the people who live outside but still want to read.

In 2011, Moulton organized a Kickstarter campaign seeking $4000 for a bike, a cart, and the ability to pay a small staff of willing street librarians. She got $5345. Joined by Diana Rempe and a host of others, Moulton began to stock her cart. "It's not just a little novelty act – 'Oh, that's so Portland and

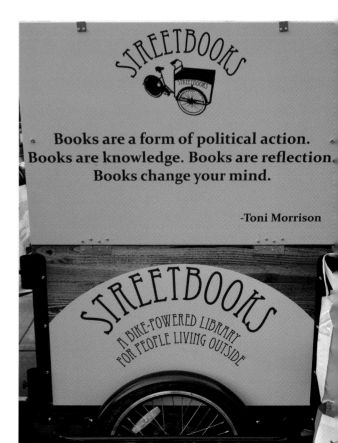

Books are a form of political action. Books are knowledge. Books are reflection. Books change your mind.

-Toni Morrison

STREETBOOKS

A BIKE-POWERED LIBRARY FOR PEOPLE LIVING OUTSIDE

cute," Rempe said in an interview with the *New York Times* in 2014. The librarians began with a simple concept: asking people they wanted to read, and then filling their cart with those titles or similar. The offerings included Spanish books on chess strategy for a pair of Cuban-born labourers waiting for jobs on the city's east side, or a copy of *Lord of the Flies* that one woman requested to loan to her friend who, she insisted, couldn't know what the world was until he read it.

Patrons of the Street Books library are given a library card, but there is no need to show proof of address or any other form of identification. To borrow a book, the librarians employ the tried-and-true system of the pre-digital library: a patron removes the card on the front flap of the book they want to borrow, signs their name upon it, and leaves it with the librarian. "There are no fees and no fines and if we don't cross paths again, we encourage folks to pass the books on to people who will enjoy them," reads a statement on their website.

The story of Street Books has been immortalized in its own publication. During the summer that Street Books began to make its first rounds under Laura Moulton's care, Ben Hodgson became a regular patron, setting a still-unbroken record for number of books borrowed in one season. He would eventually become a board member and librarian for Street Books, but in the summer of 2011, "I was there almost every week for the entire first season," he told *Al Jazeera* in 2016. "At about three books a week I probably read over fifty books that summer. Just sitting around with nothing to do but stare off into space." Then, he disappeared. Laura didn't see him again for nearly two years. The two eventually reconnected, full of questions, which led to a story, which led to *Loaners*, a street-level memoir from a community whose stories are seldom told.

LEFT Librarians sync up before a regular route. **OPPOSITE** Books are stocked based on patron requests. **BELOW** Portland's proud literary heritage keeps Street Books alive.

THE HASKELL FREE LIBRARY & OPERA HOUSE

QUEBEC, CANADA & VERMONT, USA

HOW TO FIND IT

*The Haskell has two different addresses:
93 Caswell Avenue, Derby Line, VT, USA
1 Rue Church, Stanstead, Quebec, Canada*

*US: +1 802 873 3022 and in Canada: +1 819 876 2471
haskelloperahouse.org*

The Haskell is surrounded by manicured gardens, perfect for a picnic, and a regular schedule of plays, concerts and other shows is updated on their website.

The inherent magic of a library is that it is a free space in which all people may access education, entertainment, and explorations that take them above and beyond the boundaries of where they were born. This concept is personified not just by the books within, but the very building that is the Haskell Free Library and Opera House.

A grand dame of Victorian spires and red bricks straddling the Canadian and US border (Stanstead, Quebec and Derby Line, Vermont, more specifically), the Haskell, as it is more commonly referred to, was built in 1901 under the direction of Martha Stewart Haskell. Martha was born in Canada. Her husband, Carlos Freeman Haskell, was born in the United States. Carlos, unfortunately, died in a tragic accident early in their marriage. And so it happened that, by means of his will and that of her parents, Martha Haskell found herself inheriting a massive fortune. With it, she made the decision to build something for the benefit of the Canadian-US border communities she grew up amongst – communities with few amenities, who struggled daily with over border laws that sought to tell people who could go where, when and why. These laws would only increase in strictness as time marched on. Just four years after the Haskell opened,

OPPOSITE The Haskell is a Victorian architectural gem – too pretty to remove, even though its existence violates international laws.

"A thick, black line runs down the floor of the building, through the opera theatre and the library, denoting which side of the property is Canadian, and which is American."

construction on the US-Canadian border was out-lawed. Everything from dog kennels to swing sets placed within 3m (10ft) of the invisible line between the two countries became forbidden. In 1925, that distance would increase to 8m (25ft).

The new laws made the Haskell even more precious. The building pays homage to both American and Canadian artistry, showcasing the majesty of local materials, such as rich granite from Stanstead and rare native wood from Vermont. The interior is filled with ornate Victorian treasures from the Old World: stained glass for the library reading rooms, and brilliant facades for the theatre.

The library – an elegant, wood-panelled room on the first floor – contains avenues of bookcases, Victorian fireplaces, plush sofas and one fantastically huge moose head, which keeps guard over the check-out desk. It is stocked with more than 20,000 titles in both French and English and remains open 38 hours a week to serve the communities of both Stanstead and Derby Line.

Due to its location, the Haskell is governed under a pastiche of international law. A thick, black line runs down the floor of the building, through the opera theatre and the library, denoting which side

of the property is Canadian, and which is American. Most of the bookcases and opera stage are technically located in Quebec. However, most of the theatre's actual seats are in Vermont. This situation has given rise to fond nicknames such as 'the only library in the USA with no books' and 'the only opera house in the USA with no stage'. The Haskell's main entrance is located in the US, and so, to reduce headaches, international border patrols allow all visitors – regardless of their passport – to enter using the main, US-based entrance. To get to the entrance, however, Canadian patrons are required to use a highlighted route through the pavement of rue Church on the Quebec side.

The Haskell's unorthodox location and subsequent bending of proper border crossing rules has had effects through history. During the years of former US President Donald Trump's travel bans, it became a safe haven for people who were born in so-called 'questionable countries' who were suddenly told that, wherever they happened to be in the world when bans were enacted, moving in and out of the US was now illegal. The Haskell, straddling two countries with a leftover rule allowing Canadian citizens to enter without a passport, became a refuge where families – divided up between the US and Canada on various visas – could, at least for a few moments, feel safe to be in the same room together. Due to pressure from US Homeland Security, this practice is officially discouraged by the Haskell's staff. But it is difficult not to imagine the ghost of Mrs. Haskell watching on, a touch pleased that her border-defying library was used for such purposes.

OPPOSITE Patrons can enjoy hopping between Canada and America as they peruse the stacks.

BELOW The real-life Brautigan Library is
based off of Richard Brautigan's hidden,
fictional library described in his famous
story *The Abortion*.

THE
BRAUTIGAN
LIBRARY

HOW TO FIND IT

*1511 Main Street,
Vancouver, WA
+1 360 993 5679;
cchmuseum.org/
brautigan-library*

A very small fee
is charged for
admission to help
keep the library
maintained.
Photography of
the unpublished
manuscripts
is strictly
forbidden.

VANCOUVER, WASHINGTON, USA

"This library came into being because of an overwhelming need and desire for such a place. There just simply had to be a library like this." That was how Richard Brautigan described the mysterious library featured in his 1971 novel, *The Abortion: An Historical Romance 1966*. In the novel, Brautigan writes of an introverted man studiously caring after a library of books that have never been and never will be published. It's not quite clear what the purpose of the archive is. No one is ever allowed to visit and read its contents. The librarian, however, is strapped tight to his mission: he must protect the library at all costs, and graciously receive whatever manuscripts are dropped on its doorstep, no matter how ungodly the hour, or how wretched the writer. However, in the real library inspired by Brautigan's fictional story, visitors are permitted to read as many forbidden stories as they would like.

The original Brautigan Library was founded in 1990 by writer and arts advocate Todd Lockwood in Burlington, Vermont, to bring Brautigan's enigmatic vision to life. Lockwood sent out a call for manuscript submissions – on the requirement that they had to be entirely unpublished. The library was watched over by a

network of 100 volunteers (it is unclear if they were all working at once, or one at time, but it is worth noting that in Brautigan noted of his fictional library "this place has very rapid turnover.")

The Vermont outpost of the Brautigan Library closed in 1997 due to a lack of funding, and Lockwood gathered the manuscripts into his home basement, for safekeeping. John Barber – a member of the Creative Media and Digital Culture programme at Washington State University Vancouver, who had once studied under Brautigan – heard of the library's closure in Vermont and hatched a plan to reopen the library in Brautigan's home state.

In 2010, The Brautigan Library was reopened. This time in Vancouver, Washington, inside the Clark County Historical Museum, which also happens to be Vancouver's original public library and a Carnegie library. This is brilliantly in keeping with the library in Brautigan's original story, which was based off the Presidio branch of the San Francisco Public Library – itself a Carnegie library.

"The collection spans family histories, absurd Brautigan-esque capers, DIY religious tracts and memoirs of ordinary lives," described journalist Megan Burbank in *The Seattle Times* in 2019, after her visit. "They don't feel like books at all, really, so much as the complete, unfiltered contents of other people's minds... I couldn't stop thinking of a passage from *Trout Fishing in America*, perhaps Brautigan's best-known work, that compares a bookstore to a graveyard:

'Thousands of graveyards were parked in rows like cars. Most of the books were out of print, and no one wanted to read them anymore and the people who had read the books had died or forgotten about them ...'"

WASHINGTON

DID SHE LEAVE ME ANY MONEY?

Alyce P. Cornyn-Selby

A
philosophical
comedy
about men, money, motivation,
winning strategies, architecture, nudism,
trucking, corporate assassinations, heart attacks,
sexual politics, hometown parades, Spiritual Warriors
and the dredging of Willapa Bay.

THE LIBRARIES OF THE MAYA & AZTEC

In Memoriam

MEXICO CITY, MEXICO

During the Classic period of the Maya civilization (200-900), scholars thrived. The stepped stone pyramids and lush green jungles of Palenque and Yaxchilán witnessed the rise of what many archaeologists consider the most sophisticated writing system in Mesoamerica. Scribes, whose work was seen as patronage to various gods, kept prolific records of every facet of society. Inside folding codices made from the bark of fig trees, they transcribed the latest teachings on everything from astronomy and mathematics to zoology, history and more.

For reasons that remain cloaked in mystery, these flourishing Mayan cities began to decline between 700 and 900. One theory suggests a plague or environmental disaster. Another, invasion, or a lost war. For one reason or another, the Mayans deserted their great temples and libraries, and the surviving people began to fade into the thick green of the Yucatan, many taking books with them.

OPPOSITE Stone relief of Mayan writing that has survived into the 21st century. The ancient Mayans were prolific writers, but manuscript examples are increasingly rare.

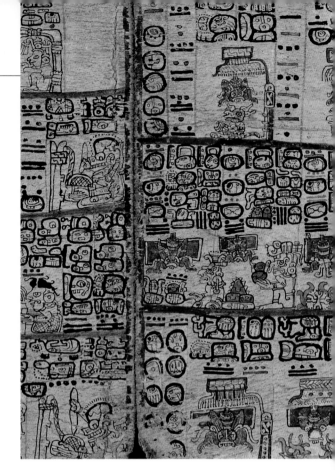

A few hundred years later, near the place that would become known as Mexico City, three great Nahua city-states – Tenochtitlán, Tlacopan and Tetzcoco – allied themselves into the Aztec Empire. Tenochtitlán was the mighty military house of the Aztecs, and its stony remains continue to be one of the most famous archaeological sites in modern Mexico. Tetzcoco, on the other hand, was revered in its time as a haven for scholars and populated with libraries.

Aztec civilization placed a high value on education for boys in all classes of society. Boys born into noble families were sent to *calmecacs*, schools where they were prepared for leadership roles with an education in history, astronomy, religion and warfare. Similarly, boys of the working class were sent to neighbourhood *tēlpochcalli* schools, where they were given lessons in agriculture, crafts and military arts, as well as language, history and religion. To support these schools and the adults they produced, every Aztec city housed numerous *amoxcalli* – a word whose most basic English translation is 'book' plus 'building.' In other words: libraries.

The most famous amoxcalli was located in Tetzcoco. This grand book building was reported to contain a vast collection of codices, many of which were preserved from before the rise of the Aztec civilization, as well as others stolen or traded from nearby cultures, such as the Maya. Tetzcoco's library was a revered safehouse for centuries of learning, as well as the wisdom gathered from the empires that came before the Aztecs. Then, catastrophe arrived.

In the 16th century, Spanish conquistadors and their clerics arrived at the shores of Mesoamerica, beginning a campaign of conquest and genocide. Between 1520 and 1525, cities fell one by one to smallpox and European cultural purity campaigns. Countless human lives were lost, as were the countless codices inside the amoxcalli. Some were taken by conquistadors back to Europe as trophies or given as gifts to noble European families. However, the vast majority were burned – never copied, or recovered.

In the Maya countryside, the notorious Spanish Franciscan priest Diego de Landa made it his mission to burn every codex he could find, seeing them as vessels for idolatry, superstition and devil worship. Maya individuals that revealed their family libraries to de Landa – private collections that contained codices dating before the downfall of Maya civilization – had them confiscated and turned into ash. From this campaign, it is generally estimated that less than 20 original Mesoamerican books have survived.

Western anthropologist Michael Coe attempts to intimate the scale of what was lost, "our knowledge of ancient Maya thought must represent only a tiny fraction of the whole picture, for of the thousands of books in which the full extent of their learning and ritual was recorded, only four have survived to modern times (as though all that posterity knew of

ourselves were to be based upon three prayer books and *Pilgrim's Progress*)."

Today, a few Maya and Aztec codices are available for public view in museums across the world. These manuscripts are under the careful watch of archivists, who understand the peril they have survived makes the wisdom they contain even more precious.

LEFT A page from the Madrid Codex, one of only three pre-Columbian Mayan books in existence. **BELOW** Mayan ruins inside the Museo Nacional de Antropologia, Mexico City.

THE WEAPON OF MASS INSTRUCTION

HOW TO FIND IT

Circulating in Buenos Aires, Argentina.

The library relies heavily on donations for fuel. If you see the library, consider tipping generously.

BUENOS AIRES, ARGENTINA

This is not your average book mobile.

Education is commonly seen as the key barrier to war. The argument being that if we have the means and desire to educate our minds, we will be more resistant to senseless violence and the manipulations of propaganda. Empathy is generated when we see the world from another person's eyes – hearing their stories, relating to their troubles. It is hard to go to war with someone if you can relate to their story.

The idea that education is the antidote to destruction has been brought to life in Argentina, by artist, poet and bibliophile Raul Lemesoff. It is called the Weapon of Mass Instruction (Arma de Instruccion Masiva), although it is occasionally referred to as the Think Tank. Lemesoff began the project by taking the body of a 1979 Ford Falcon – the vehicle favoured by Argentinian dictator, General Videla, to kidnap students, reporters and anyone else whose opinions threatened the regime. In Buenos Aires in 1979, if you saw someone pushed inside a dark green Ford Falcon driven by Videla's spies, you would not see them come back out again.

This was the car Raul Lemesoff chose to build a library out of. His aim: to transform the symbol of evil into a vessel of peace, delivering books far and wide – so that dictatorships never take hold again.

After four years of welding, hammering and engine work, he transformed the Falcon into the image of a classic, army green tank, complete with swivel turret and a lengthy gun barrel. The engine gurgles and churns like a true machine of war. The major difference, however, is noticed right away: the skeleton of the vehicle may be a war tank, but its flesh is made of paper.

The Weapon of Mass Instruction is stocked with 900 titles of donated, used books. Subjects range from scientific essays, poetry anthologies, novels, memoirs, children's stories and more. Raul has taken the tank around Buenos Aires on 'missions;' that is, thrusting books into the hands of strangers at bus stops, pulling up to playgrounds and insisting families grab whatever interests them, and collecting donated books to further line the body of the tank. His main goal is reaching kids, especially those in remote areas of Argentina, where up to 50% do not attend school.

It is not an idyllic, tidy library, where everything is coded according to the Dewey decimal system, where stern librarians shush anyone who gets too excited. If it were, Raul himself would probably get thrown out. He is bombastic, eccentric, excited. This library is the opposite of silent tyranny; it is a chaotic, gurgling beast of education and free love, captained by a mad wizard. Raul wants to make a "mess of people's heads," forcing readers to question their assumptions. In a 2014 video profiling the library, produced by 7UP, a friend once described him as being "very unwell adjusted to this society."

Raul has since made two more book tanks to join the original, which spend their days circulating Buenos Aires.

THE BIBLIOBURRO

MAGDALENA VALLEY, COLOMBIA

HOW TO FIND IT

The Biblioburro operates within the Magdalena Valley, near Colombia's Caribbean coast. www.instagram.com/ biblioburro_oficial

Luis Soriano's story, and the magic of the Magdelena Valley, are detailed in Jordan Salama's book *Every Day the River Changes*.

Luis Soriano, referred to by his neighbours as 'Prof' or 'Doctor', grew up playing in the green fields of the Magdalena Valley in Colombia. His parents – hard-working farmers – never ceased to remind their children about the value of an education. Growing up in the countryside, Soriano learned to read the land: that a speedy line of ants meant drenching rains would soon come, or that the rapid hush of night frogs meant someone was moving in the darkness.

In the 1970s, intensifying violence gripped the Magdalena valley. Paramilitaries and criminal groups kidnapped children, lit cars on fire, and tortured ranchers. They especially targeted schoolteachers, who they saw as a threat to their political philosophies. Soriano's parents were compelled to send him and his siblings to the city to finish high school. But when Soriano graduated, he made the choice to return to the Magdalena Valley and become a schoolteacher himself.

After a short time in charge of his classroom, he noticed a problem: none of his students did any of their schoolwork. In fact, they seemed to not be making any progress at all. He realized why: many of them simply could not read, or at least not read well. Most lived on isolated rural farms, some without electricity. The families worked hard, but most did not own books, let alone have the time to read them. So, in 1997, he decided to bring books to them.

OPPOSITE Luis Soriano understood that a donkey was a more effective means of getting books to children than any other medium.

© Jordan Salama

The narrow, backcountry roads along the Magdalena Valley were not built for cars at this point. But donkeys – whose slim hooves and agile legs could easily navigate both the mud of the wet season, and the foreboding heat of the dry season – were made for the terrain.

Soriano acquired one donkey, and then, realizing he needed more book storage, another. He named them Alfa and Beto, for *alfabeto* (the Spanish word for alphabet). The man and the two book-laden donkeys began their journey before dawn, stopping at the homes of each one of his students to sit and read with them, and lend them whatever book they enjoyed, so they could practice on their own, later. Soriano's project became known as The Biblioburro.

In 2003, Juan Gossaín (a popular Colombian radio host) heard of the Biblioburro and shared it with his listeners. Book donations poured in. Over two decades later, the Biblioburro is now home to thousands of titles and over 20 travelling donkey libraries. Luis was able to open the first primary school and permanent public library in La Gloria (his hometown), stocked with computers and flat-screen televisions, and loaded with books from around the world. He went on to found three other schools in the broader Magdalena valley, with the Biblioburro working in conjunction with them all. The library has expanded into Biblioburro Digital, which brings laptops, tablets, and other technologies to children living in rural farm communities, and Biblioburro Very Well, an English-language education programme.

Soriano, now in his 40s, is still in charge of the project. When he approaches a farmstead, the children often run out to greet him, jumping and

"Without fail, twice a week in the soft pre-dawn light, Soriano takes his donkeys through the rugged landscape to the children in the Magdalena valley, some of whom still live without electricity, to read them stories, and lend them books."

smiling, excited for story time. He has endured harassment from paramilitaries and been tied to a tree by thieves. His gait has a permanent limp, the result of a bone-shattering fall from Alfa's back many years ago. Nevertheless, without fail, twice a week in the soft pre-dawn light, Soriano takes his donkeys through the rugged landscape to the children in the Magdalena valley, some of whom still live without electricity, to read them stories, and lend them books.

LEFT The residents of the Magdalena Valley honor the Biblioburro with a mural. **BELOW** A group of children lean in during the Biblioburro's regular story time.

BELOW Jose Alberto Gutierrez's library is made entirely from books previously hidden in trash cans. **OPPOSITE** Bogota's Nueva Gloria neighborhood has no public libraries.

THE STRENGTH OF WORDS

BOGOTÁ, COLOMBIA

HOW TO FIND IT

Calle 47A Sur No 8A Este, Bogotá, Colombia +57 313 2867352; facebook.com/ fundacionlafuerzadelas- palabras

The library (which is to say, Gutierrez's house) is typically only open to the public on weekends. Gutierrez's work was immortalized in a children's book of its own: *Digging for Words*, by Angela Burke Kunkel.

When we think of a hidden library, we might think of something quirky; something with an element of preposterousness that lends a certain charm to every book tucked inside. However, the most hidden places on Earth are not always charming. Sometimes, they are the places we'd prefer not to think about. For example: the insides of rubbish bins.

Seven million people live in Colombia's capital, and for all of them, there are 13 libraries (by comparison, London, a city of just under nine million, is served by 325). Jose Alberto Gutierrez lives in Nueva Gloria, a neighbourhood in South Bogotá, where housing is dense and resources are scarce. He says there aren't a lot of places for kids to play, let alone do their homework, or get their hands on a book. This is perhaps why, when Gutierrez started noticing books turning up in the rubbish he collected in the richer neighbourhoods each week, he was offended. "People often wander about without dreams, when they don't know about books," Gutierrez reflected to *CGTN TV* in 2017. "But after you start reading and get to know literature, you not only discover the world, but you learn how to help others. And in my case, I discovered that this was my mission in life. This is why I came into the world. This is what makes me really happy."

It began with a copy of *Anna Karenina* that Gutierrez found in 1995, in a rubbish bin in Bogotá's Bolivar neighbourhood. After that, he began to notice more books, and, instead of tossing them into the back of the truck's garbage bay, he tossed them into the driver's seat. "I was surprised to find books in the trash I was collecting," he said. "Suddenly, it made my job really interesting. I began waking up earlier, so I could be more alert in looking for them. Every day, I brought home a backpack full of them."

He took the books to the only location he knew they'd be safe: his house. From there, the entire family became involved in the project, his wife helping to select, clean and repair the books he found, and his daughter acting as junior library assistant. Gutierrez named the house-library La Fuerza de las Palabras (The Strength of Words).

Word got out about the refuse collector-turned-librarian, and soon, Gutierrez began to notice tidy stacks of books next to the rubbish bins he collected, earning the nickname 'Lord of the Books'. Today, he has over 30,000 titles stacked in his house, ranging from textbooks to picture books – all collected from the rubbish. The library primarily serves children, who come in to explore stories, do their homework, or just enjoy a quiet place to daydream.

"This place is very important to me," said Natalie Ordus to *CGTN*, a Nueva Gloria resident who has been frequenting the library since she was ten. "It gives us a wealth of knowledge, so we can experiment and learn. Books teach you to see life in a different way."

BELOW Muyinga's first library caters
mostly to deaf patrons. **OPPOSITE** Hammocks
are hung from the roof of the library,
making for a cosy reading session.

LIBRARY OF MUYINGA

MUYINGA, BURUNDI

HOW TO FIND IT

48WP+H44,
Muyinga, Burundi

The library is
part of a future
school for deaf
children, in the
process of being
developed by BC
architects and the
diocese of Muyinga
Odedim.

Burundi has a rich oral tradition, passing information person to person, creating a shared identity through storytelling. Which is to say, people talk a lot more than they write. You get the wisdom you need from your elders and friends, rather than sitting alone in silence, staring at a book. Storytellers abound, but the opposite is true for libraries. This isn't really a problem – unless you are deaf.

For centuries, deaf children in Burundi found themselves cut off from society, education, and friendships that can come with both. These children ended up isolated unless someone took the time to teach them sign language. This was the problem the Library of Muyinga sought to solve.

Muyinga is one of Burundi's largest cities. Despite its size, it lacked a single library. But in 2012, a high school director, a bishop for the local church, a nun, a foreman, 40 labourers, an NGO worker, several teachers, a Belgian architecture firm, and a few hundred deaf Burundi children and their parents – all got together to build one.

The budget was small, the selection of natural resources challenging. But, materials and machinery like virgin wood and bulldozers were not needed, thanks to the long-standing Burundian technique of building with brick and clay.

BELOW The library's windows function as open and closed signs. OPPOSITE Books are stocked based on patrons' tastes.

The Belgian architecture firm brought their software, their measuring tools, and their eager interns ready to get their hands dirty. They met with local Burundian architects to understand the materials, techniques and building typologies. Burundi craftsmen taught them about compressed-brick production, and how to weave sisal into rope strong enough to support the library's signature central hammock.

The finished library resembles a souped-up Muyinga house – with a long, extra-wide porch for resting, visiting with friends, and reading in the shade. Transparent doors lead between the library's inside and outside. Fully opened, they reveal the adjacent square and an arresting view of Burundi's *milles collines* (1000 hills). They also function as an 'open/closed' sign letting any who approach know if the library is open for business.

In the centre of the library, a giant hammock made from sisal rope hangs from the ceiling. Up to three children can pile in, swapping books back and forth, between long periods of silent reading.

ST CATHERINE'S MONASTERY LIBRARY

SINAI, EGYPT

HOW TO FIND IT

Saint Catherine, South Sinai Governorate 8730070, Egypt
sinaimonastery.com

St Catherine's is an active monastery and offers visitors guided tours through the library, as well as the chapel, refectory, kitchen, cells and gardens. The entire top floor of the south wing of the library has been renovated to create conservation workshops and digital photography studios, improve storage for the books and manuscripts, and provide reading space for visiting scholars.

"The place on which you are standing is holy ground." These were the words famously spoken by God to Moses when the prophet came upon the burning bush in the Sinai desert. In Deuteronomy 32:10, however, Sinai is also described as "the waste, howling wilderness". This section of the Egyptian peninsula is a land of sun-baked rocks, barren horizons, and sawtooth mountains. Nevertheless, or perhaps precisely because of the foreboding landscape, 3rd- and 4th-century hermits made their way here, to find solitude and contemplate the mysteries of God.

In the 6th century, Byzantine emperor Justinian commissioned St Catherine's Monastery to be built around the supposed location of the biblical burning bush. As generations passed, Egypt was invaded by scores of armies, from 7th-century Arab conquerors to 19th-century French imperialists. All agreed to leave St Catherine's in peace, as if understanding that it operated outside the affairs of mortal men. Perhaps because it was so hidden between the rocks, perhaps because it was blessed, the Sinai monastery has never been destroyed or abandoned, regardless of what wars raged in the lands surrounding it.

Thousands of people continue to make the trek to Sinai every year, following in the footsteps of 1700 years worth of pilgrims. Most people who visit Sinai do so to climb the mountain where Moses was said to have received the tablets of the

OPPOSITE Thousands of pilgrims still travel to Mt Sinai every year to watch the sunrise. Many, however, walk past the 1500 year old monastery and its cache of books.

Ten Commandments, or to pay homage at the well where he met his wife, Zipporah. The monastery's library is not often the highlight, tucked away in an old stone building south of the Church of the Transfiguration, behind a red door. But it is a treasure trove of rare books and manuscripts.

Since its inception, St Catherine's was reported by passing sages as an excellent holding ground for sacred texts, thanks to the dry and stable climate of the Sinai Peninsula, and the relative isolation of the monastery itself. The oldest texts in the library date back to the 4th century, here to rest forever after an arduous journey through the surrounding deserts.

The library today contains 3300 manuscripts in the Old Collection, as well as a series of manuscripts that came to light in 1975, known as the New Finds. Many of them contain glorious illuminations, painted over the course of years by devoted monks. The languages featured in the library reflect those who made the journey here – including classical Greek, Arabic, Syriac, Georgian, and Slavonic – and contain topics ranging from religion to geography and medicine.

One hundred and sixty manuscripts in the library are palimpsests, meaning that they have been reused. Written on animal skin parchments, Monks erased the previous content from these in order to write something new. Twenty-first century scholars are able to study these manuscripts with multispectral imaging, to glean both the newer text, and what the monk thought worth erasing behind it. The library's most important palimpsest is the *Codex Sinaiticus* – a late 4th century, nearly-complete translation of the four canonical Gospels of the New Testament into Syriac Aramaic – the main literary language used at the very beginning of Christianity. This palimpsest is the oldest copy of the Gospels in Syriac. Put simply: the earliest manuscript of the Bible anyone has ever found.

"A few of the Sinai manuscripts are splendid works of art, with gilded letters and brilliant illuminations, created in Constantinople in the tenth, eleventh, and twelfth centuries, when the City was at its height as

"The oldest texts in the library date back to the 4th century, here to rest forever after an arduous journey through the surrounding deserts."

the centre of culture and devotion," says Father Justin of Sinai, Librarian of St Catherine's Monastery, on the Sinai Palimpsests Project website, "But no less significant are the humble manuscripts written at Sinai, often on reused parchment, bound between rough boards, the pages stained from long use, a witness to the deprivations and austerity of Sinai, and to the generations of monks who have maintained the life of devotion and the cycle of daily services at this holy place".

LEFT St Catherine's has one of the richest collections of ancient manuscripts in the world, rivaling the Vatican. **BELOW** The monastery has always been granted protection by passing conquerers.

BELOW After situating his horse, Librarian
Legesse Janfa prepares to read to a group
of children.

THE HORSE LIBRARY

HAWASSA, ETHIOPIA

Mobile libraries are employed across the globe to deliver books to those who live in remote areas — especially children. However, the most effective form of mobile transport for those books depends on the terrain the librarian has to cross. In Ethiopia, after attempting cars, motorcycles and even donkeys, it was eventually discovered that horses are the best fit for navigating the countryside, where the roadless landscape often necessitates crossing a mix of seasonal rivers, high-elevation plateaus, and arid lowlands. So, that is the technology the Ethiopia Reads organization puts to work.

The non-profit was cofounded by Jane Kurtz, an Ethiopian American children's librarian at the San Francisco Public Library, and Yohannes Gebregeorgis, a children's book writer. "They both grew up in rural parts of Ethiopia," described Malcolm Clark, Board President of Ethiopia Reads, "so they understood the land and what the people are dealing with on the ground." Many parents desired to give their children the opportunities that came with reading, but there were obstacles: it would take too much time to send children away to the library, when they were needed at home to help with the demanding schedule of farmwork. Not to mention, the journey itself was extremely dangerous for a child on foot. "Ethiopia has an ancient history of writing culture," noted Malcolm, "but it was reserved for religious leaders and dedicated scholars." As of 2024, only 49% of Ethiopia's adult population was literate.

HOW TO FIND IT

Like all mobile libraries, the Horse Library has no fixed address. If you want to visit on the ground, contact Ethiopia Reads to find the latest location of the mobile donkey library in Hawassa, and the latest schedule for the horse libraries.
+251 612 354 2184;
ethiopiareads.org

Ethiopia Reads hosts the largest professional children's reading conference in Ethiopia every year, usually held in Addis Ababa, to motivate more people to join the cause.

"The routes are fixed, so children
know to look for the bright colours of
the horse on the horizon, and run to
welcome them into the village."

Ethiopia Reads began by building a children's public library in Addis Ababa, the capital, and a year or two later in Hawassa, a major city in Ethiopia's Great Rift Valley. Eventually, for the children who couldn't make it to the Hawassa Reading Centre, they offered another option: a cart on four wheels, full of books, pulled by two donkeys, which visited various neighbourhoods. "It gets a lot of attention," said Malcolm, "we still have it moving around the centre of town, and we will be starting another one." The donkeys seemed not to tolerate the long distances required to reach the more remote sections of the countryside, however. "Horses, it turns out, are much better for very rural places with no or poor roads," said Malcolm.

The librarian's horses are fitted with circus-tent-pattern saddles, which they fill with stacks and stacks of children's books. The pair then travels into the deeper recesses of the countryside, often for the entire day. The routes are fixed, so children know to look for the bright colours of the horse on the horizon and run to welcome them into the village.

"Today, we have three horse mobile libraries, used in the countryside, and soon we will have two donkey mobile libraries in Hawassa all primarily for after school reading," commented Malcolm.

According to one of the horse librarians, Nagassa Jaffar, the most rewarding thing he experienced on his routes was seeing individual children improve their reading skills over time, some going from being unable to recognize letters, to handling entire books on their own.

A major issue faced by the NGO has been the shortage of books written in the languages that the children hear at home. "Ethiopia – and the world – had very few children's books in Amharic, the national language, let alone the other major mother tongue languages" continued Malcolm. "Even if you have a motivated parent, it's just hard for them to find books their child would understand. A huge part of our work involves supporting publishing initiatives in Ethiopia to create more books, designed from the start to be easily translated into any one of Ethiopia's 12 major languages."

In 2020 the brutal Tigray War began, inflicting widespread destruction upon the Ethiopian countryside. By 2021, 5.1 million people were displaced from their homes and livelihoods. "We never hear about the scale of the casualties and human displacement," said Malcolm. "There's still about 4 million people who are displaced, many of whom are children, and many more in conflict-devastated communities. They can't go to school anymore; their education has been interrupted. And they would enjoy a little comfort, a little distraction." Ethiopia Reads has printed and distributed over 45,000 books in three Ethiopian languages to refugees and plans to donate another 300,000 in the coming years. The 80 school libraries still stand, eagerly awaiting the return of their students.

OPPOSITE Equines make for ideal mobile libraries in the rugged, arid landscape of rural Ethiopia.

BELOW Librarian Rashid Farah leads a camel carrying books to a primary school in Garissa. **OPPOSITE** Two girls sample books from the Camel Library.

THE CAMEL LIBRARY

In Memoriam

KENYA, AFRICA

If you imagine that bookish desert nomads have trouble accessing libraries, you would not be wrong. However, in the rural village of Garissa, Kenya, in 1996, a librarian had a bright idea to remedy the problem. What if, similar to the horse-drawn wagons of the Great Depression that delivered books to rural readers across the US, a roving library could serve the nomadic desert tribes of Kenya?

Every morning the Kenyan Library Service prepared three camels for travel. The party consisted of a librarian in charge, two assistants and a skilled camel herdsman who knew how to keep the moody beasts in check. One camel was tasked with carrying a whopping 400 books. Another was packed with a tent, reading mat and chairs. These librarians and animals regularly worked until nightfall, ranging 11 km (7 miles) in any direction from their home base, Monday through Thursday.

Once the caravan arrived at a village of nomads, the mat was spread, the tent (or pop-up library) was pitched, and the books were laid out. In no time, the mat was happily crowded, with children engrossed in picture books and adults reading up on reference materials. At the end of the day, everything was loaded back onto the camels, which headed back to

BELOW The human-camel team are often out all day, traveling between remote villages. OPPOSITE A group of children patiently wait to explore the camel library's offerings that day.

the library in preparation for the next day's journey to a different part of the region. Each patron was allowed to borrow two books and had 14 days before the camels returned, at which time the books could be renewed or returned.

The library eventually grew to 3500 customers – far more than your average rural library. The service was particularly valuable to nearby schools, as it often provided books that appeared on school syllabuses. However, there were challenges. If a camel fell ill, the service was disrupted. During the summer months, the hot travel proved brutal. Ultimately, The Kenya National Library decided the special service was too expensive to maintain; it relieved the camels of duty and replaced them with motorcycles once the roads in the region were improved.

In other parts of the world, however, camels remain a critical component in getting books to children. During the height of the Covid pandemic, when schools were closed for public safety, India's International Reading Campaign initiated a programme

in Rajasthan to bring books to children at home. Especially in outlying areas where internet connections are sparse, and remote learning is not a practical option, parents began to worry about their children losing progress in reading, and becoming bored. The programme leaders gathered 1500 books into a balloon-bedecked cart and hitched it to the backs of camels, whose sure-footed steps could handle the sandy, slippery landscapes surrounding Jodhpur far better than the average car.

Accompanying the cart were a member of the NGO, a local teacher, and a few community members who offered reading assistance, storytime, and once again connected children with stories that made their eyes light up. A similar programme in Pakistan, run by the Alif Laila Book Bus Society, focuses on bringing books to girls in Balochistan, where female literacy remains half of the male rate. The patient camels deliver books to girls at home, where they can revel in stories regardless of access to a local school.

THE TIMBUKTU MANUSCRIPTS

DJENNE, MALI

HOW TO FIND IT

The library does not have a fixed address but is in a well-marked building directly across from the Grand Mosqueé in Djenne. +223 78 44 84 94; facebook.com/ DjenneManuscriptLibrary

Parts of Mali are considered dangerous for outsiders to visit. Please check local conditions before planning your trip. Also, the public portion of the Djenne Manuscript Library is under frequent threat of closure due to funding concerns. Consider donating if you visit.

When Europe was deep in the anti-intellectual throes of the Dark Ages, the Songhai Empire was a blossoming scholar's paradise in West Africa. Timbuktu was the place where learned men gathered to debate law, expound scientific theories, create art and trade books. The Sankoré, Djingareyber and Sidi Yahiya mosques hosted up to 25,000 academics, merchants of gold and salt flooded the city with wealth, and scribes produced manuscripts by the thousands, with topics ranging from medicine and mathematics to music and sex.

As with most grand empires, Songhai eventually fell to the designs of neighbouring conquerors. However, its libraries were not burned. Most of the manuscripts were taken away by individuals, where they were incorporated into private family libraries, and passed down from generation to generation. These diasporic literary treasures became known collectively as the Timbuktu Manuscripts.

In 2007, librarians and historians began to ask their neighbours about the old books in their basements. Scrolls of swirling calligraphy and dazzling illuminations revealed love stories, astrological charts, letters between traders, and lessons in Andulsian music. One even cautioned young scientists to be wary of the corrupting power of politics. Over 150,000 manuscripts were surfaced, some from as early as the 13th century, but most historians believe this is a mere fraction of what is hiding beneath Mali's whispering sand dunes. Furthermore, many families did not wish to reveal their treasured heirlooms to strangers, for fear they would be asked to give them up – which is precisely what the historians were requesting.

OPPOSITE The front entrance to the Bibliotheque des Manuscrits al-Wangari in Mali.

"It is through these writings that we can really know our place in history," said Abdramane Ben Essayouti, Imam of Timbuktu's oldest mosque, to *Reuters* in 2007. The goal was to study and preserve the precious texts in modern research facilities and make visible their cultural wealth in public libraries.

Then, in 2012, Islamic militant groups began increasing their reach in Mali. These fundamentalists did not see the literary heritage of the Songhai Empire as a source of pride, but instead as idolatry, contradicting their version of Islam. A cultural purity campaign began. The librarians – well-read in history – knew what would come next. On 28 January 2013, Islamists came to the Ahmed Baba Institute of Higher Learning and Islamic Research, flung 4000 ancient manuscripts outside, doused them in gasoline, and set them ablaze.

This is how librarian Abdel Kader Haidara, head of the Ahmed Baba Institute, became a smuggler. Haidara had already spent over a decade as a modern-day version of a medieval book trader, travelling by camel through the desert, chartering riverboats, and hiking from village to village, to meet the families guarding these heirloom texts – and convincing them to donate them. Now, he was working in reverse.

Each night, a cadre of books were stolen away into nondescript trunks, which were then packed

into mule carts, and taken at an intentionally slow, inconspicuous pace pace to private homes. There, Haidara hoped, the books could safely wait out this dark period of Timbuktu's history. The team successfully rescued 350,000 manuscripts from the perils of fundamentalism.

A decade later, some of the manuscripts have returned to the Ahmed Baba Institute, but the vast majority are in climate-controlled storage rooms in

"Over 150,000 manuscripts were surfaced, some from as early as the 13th century, but most historians believe this is a mere fraction of what is hiding beneath Mali's whispering sand dunes."

hidden locations in Bamako, still sealed with a promise to return them once their security can be guaranteed.

In the meantime, a team of historians are working to digitize the the Timbuktu Manuscripts that have been recovered, and there are a few places you can glimpse a small portion of them across Mali. One of the best is perhaps at the Manuscript Library in Djenne, whose collection contains thousands of manuscripts from the 16th through the 19th centuries, written in Arabic, Fulfulde, Bozo and Songhai.

LEFT Timbuktu's librarians have been carefully collecting ancient manuscripts from private families for years. **BELOW** In 2012, manuscripts were smuggled out in chests to escape the torches of fundamentalists.

BELOW Librarian Saif al Islam prepares
to show a very old, miniature book.
OPPOSITE Many of Chinguetti's libraries are
private, family-owned collections that have
been passed down generations.

THE LIBRARIES OF CHINGUETTI

CHINGUETTI, MAURITANIA

HOW TO FIND IT

In rural Mauritania, most things are booked verbally on the ground. Chinguetti has several tourist lodgings, and the libraries are a common attraction, although only a few are open to the public. Saif al Islam al Ahmed Mahmoud is one of the librarians more welcoming to tourists.

The vast, arid dunes of the deep Sahara make urban development difficult, if not outright impossible. Sometimes, the only thing you can see for miles amidst the mountains of sand is the road that brought you there, if that. This makes the bygone civilizations that have thrived here even more remarkable.

The small, stone village of Chinguetti was founded in 777 by Berber merchants as a trading post. The umber-walled fortress was home to a maze of labyrinthine alleys and doors carved from ancient acacia trees. Chinguetti grew over the centuries, eventually coming under the control of the Almoravid dynasty and evolving into a landmark stop on trans-Saharan trade routes. Merchants from present-day Senegal to Andalucia convened here to exchange ivory, fabrics, spices and knowledge. Chinguetti's Rue des Savants (street of intelligent ones) gained fame as a gathering place for students, Imams and pilgrims on their way to and from Mecca to stop and debate the finer points of Islamic law. Sometimes, these sages left books behind.

By the Middle Ages, the fortified stone walls of Chinguetti were housing hundreds of manuscripts in dozens of privately-owned libraries, with families acting as librarians. Travelling scholars would continue to stop here to study Quranic law, astronomy,

mathematics, poetry, philosophy, medicine, governance and more. As the centuries progressed, the camel and horse-drawn trade routes of the Sahara faded into the past. However, the bones of this scholarly oasis in the middle of the desert remain firmly intact. A population of nearly 5000 people still live in Chinguetti, between the new town and the old town. And the books the sages left behind centuries ago are still here.

Today, Chinguetti has 13 libraries, containing over 6000 texts, some dating as far back as the 9th century. The books contain a wealth of knowledge on science, poetry and Quranic law, along with historic legal decrees, civil contracts and bills of sale from the traders who did business in Chinguetti. Many of the manuscripts are family heirlooms, donated to larger libraries for protection and research. Some of them were written on gazelle skin and bound in goat hide, wrapped in bamboo tubes or hand spun fabric and tucked into stone shelves. The family library of Mohammed Habbot – considered one of the oldest libraries in the world for Islamic scholarship – has over 1600 manuscripts stored in iron cabinets, adjacent to reading desks.

The custodians of these libraries keep the tradition of passing down their care to family members and trusted scholars. Foreign curators have asked to relocate the manuscripts to more controlled environments, but the librarians are reluctant and unimpressed by the offers. "It's impossible to give up your house, your leg, or your eye and preserve them at the same time," said Saif al Islam al Ahmed Mahmoud to *The Washington Post* in 2023. His library in Chinguetti houses over 700 manuscripts, collected, donated and cared for by his family over centuries. "This is our inheritance."

Overall, the dry desert air and dedication of the librarians have helped preserve the fragile volumes. Tourists are welcome into the libraries by private appointment, but whether you can actually view the books will be up to the librarian. The texts are usually only permitted to be touched by historians, and scholars who still visit Chinguetti to study ancient Islamic Law.

In recognition of its historical significance, Chinguetti has been awarded the title of a UNESCO world heritage site, which adds further protections to its timeless treasures.

HEYDAR ALIYEV INTERNATIONAL AIRPORT LIBRARY

HOW TO FIND IT

Heydar Aliyev International Airport, Airport Highway AZ1044 Baku, Azerbaijan +994 12 497 27 27; airport.az

The library accepts donations if you need to unload a book or two from your suitcase.

BAKU, AZERBAIJAN

If you look up a list of libraries in the city of Baku, Azerbaijan – many of them ancient, prestigious, architectural gems – you will not find The Heydar Aliyev International Airport Library. Perhaps that's because it's hard to pin down: it exists between 'where you are' and 'where you're going', in a way station of time, otherwise known as an airport terminal.

Turkish design group Autoban conceived the entire terminal for comfort, and the library is one of several 'cocoons' – wooden droplets the size of houses – that break the place into cozy compartments.

By using wood, stone and textiles as the primary materials, along with carefully composed soft lighting, Autoban sought to create a tactile and soothing environment for travellers – people who are so often weary, anxious, and running on an insufficient amount of sleep. Creature comforts found inside the wooden cocoons include airport standards like cafes, newsagents and gift shops. However, one is, to the frequent surprise of those who stumble into it, a library – a place most of us associate with calm, imagination, distraction, and perhaps the happiest parts of our childhood.

OPPOSITE The library cocoon at the Baku airport awaits travelers in need of a good story.

The library takes up two storeys, with a spiral staircase resembling a swirling white ribbon connecting the levels. The airport stocks the books with titles, but patrons travelling through may also unload a title or two from their luggage. The result is a library whose books come from cultures you may have never encountered, languages you may have never seen, and perhaps, the occasional flash of a bestseller from your own home turf. The books sit in open-plan shelves, easy to peruse from two sides, with nearby plush chairs and tables welcoming you to stay a while (notably, the cafe right across the way sells ice cream).

The design fits nicely with Baku's reputation as an architectural wonderland. The capital and largest city in Azerbaijan, Baku has spent the first part of the 21st century positioning itself as the country that changes it skyline every few years, producing skyscrapers that look like giant metallic petals and sparkling concert arenas that resemble crystal palaces. The library is 100% free, a silent agreement between people amid great transition, returning from or heading towards a new world, swapping stories inside the way station of reality.

BELOW The nine story entrance of the Mogao Caves in Dunhuang. **OPPOSITE** Sinologist Paul Pelliot examines forgotten scrolls in the unearthed 'library cave' in 1908.

THE MOGAO GROTTOES

DUNHUANG, CHINA

HOW TO FIND IT

The Mogao Grottoes are about 30 minutes south of downtown Dunhuang, but tours start and end at the visitor centre, which is near the train station.
+86 937 886 9060

The library cave is permitted to view only by ticketed people as part of a group tour of several caves.

Connecting the farthest reaches of China, through West Asia, and into the heart of Arabia, the Silk Road facilitated global trade of precious fabrics, camels, wine, perfume, gunpowder and porcelain – but also of stories, made solid in books, passed from hand to hand by traders.

Dunhuang was also a centre for Buddhist meditation, pilgrimage and worship. In the year 366, monks began to dig caves into the surrounding mountains of their oasis. These caves served as rooms for prayer and ceremony, but also storehouses for art, manuscripts and treasures collected from all the traders who passed through Dunhuang. Over 500 hundred caves in total would eventually be dug, known today as the either Mogao Grottoes, or more commonly in Chinese, the Caves of the Thousand Buddhas.

One of these ancient caves came to be known by future archaeologists as Cave 17 or, more commonly, the Hidden Library Cave. Although pilgrims and treasures seemed to flow easily in and out of the caves' hundreds of chambers, the library was different. In the 11th century, for reasons that continue to confound archaeologists, someone decided it needed to be closed, permanently. The library was sealed up behind stone walls, leaving the volumes within to sit

in complete darkness, forgotten, as centuries of conquest, revolution and trade ticked by around them. Then in 1900, someone broke in.

Dunhuang had lost its prominence over the years as the Silk Road declined in usage. Nevertheless, Taoist monk Wang Yuanlu was on a campaign to restore the neglected caves to their former glory. One day, while clearing away sand clogged corridors, he followed the drifting odour from a cigarette to an area that he realized he had mistaken for airtight. He broke down the stone and found himself staring into a room no one had set eyes on in over 700 years. The discovery of the library would later be lauded as one of the greatest archaeological finds of the 20th century, on par with the tomb of Tutankhamun.

Wang would eventually show the cave to Hungarian-British archaeologist Aurel Stein, who would describe his first glimpse of this literary treasure cave thusly: "Heaped up in layers, but without any order, there appeared in the dim light of the priest's little lamp a solid mass of manuscript bundles rising to a height of nearly ten feet, and filling, as subsequent measurement showed, close on 500 cubic feet. The area left clear within the room was just sufficient for two people to stand in."

The estimated 50,000 manuscripts ranged in age from the 5th century to the early 11th and were written in Chinese, Tibetan, Old Uyghur, Sanskrit, Sogdian, Khotanese, Hebrew and more. Paper scrolls, Tibetan palm-leaf manuscripts, and faded paintings on hemp, silk and paper revealed Buddhist sutras and scriptural commentaries, as well as apocryphal Christian documents, Confucian writings, and Taoist canons. Detailed records depict everyday life of past Buddhist monks, including administrative documents, politics, anthologies, glossaries, dictionaries, and even calligraphic exercises and music scores. One particularly notable treasure was unearthed:

The Diamond Sutra, which would come to be dated to 868 – the oldest physical book ever discovered.

Wang would eventually sell Stein, as well as archaeologist Paul Pelliot, thousands of the priceless manuscripts for less than £300 (about £30,000 today). The European men transported most of them carefully back to their European homelands before scholars in Beijing halted the plunder in 1910. Most of the remaining manuscripts were taken to Beijing and now reside under the studious watch of the caretakers inside the National Library of China. The documents that were purchased by Pelliot and Stein reside in such institutions as the British Library and the Bibliothèque Nationale de France. Several manuscripts remained in Dunhuang, stored in libraries and museums. In the 1990s, historians from across the globe agreed to band together to digitize these

treasures as part of the International Dunhuang Project, and this catalogue is free to access online. However, there are still rumours that, upon Wang's discovery in 1900, residents of Dunhuang entered the caves and stole away unknown quantities of manuscripts. To this day, we cannot be entirely sure how many literary treasures inside of the Mogao Grottoes have actually been brought to light.

LEFT Dunhuang's large oasis made it a popular stop with traders along the silk road.
BELOW Ancient Buddhist monks built caves into the desert rock to store artifacts and books.

VENDING MACHINE LIBRARIES

HOW TO FIND IT

Across Shenzhen, a map can be found at www.sz.gov.cn/ en_szgov/life/cultural/ libraries/content/ post_10791995.html. szlib.org.cn

There are hundreds of vending machine libraries across China, many now allowing you to preorder a book and pick it up at the machine within 48 hours.

SHENZHEN, CHINA

China's Shenzhen public library system has made accessing free books as convenient as getting a can of Coke. That is to say, they put them in vending machines.

Technically, book vending machines got their start in 1937 London, with a device going by the delightful name of the Penguincubator. The machine offered customers rapid access to cheap Penguin paperbacks at a time when bookstores were not commonly found in shopping districts. The concept of book vending machines spread to other countries, perhaps most famously in Japan, where as early as the 1970s and 1980s, you could quench your thirst for new manga at any time of day through comic book vending machines. In the 2000s, in France, affordable bookseller Maxi Livres introduced book vending machines to train stations, providing commuters with smart titles to make the ride pass faster.

The key difference between a book vending machine and a book library, of course, is the same as the difference between a brick-and-mortar bookstore and a brick-and-mortar library: one sells books in exchange for money, while the other simply says, 'Just bring it back, please'.

While Shenzhen was the first city to introduce them, today, vending machine libraries are fairly common across China – in subway stations, airport terminals, and generally, wherever people congregate. In Beijing's Chaoyang district, vending machine libraries accounted for nearly a third of all borrowed books in

OPPOSITE Vending machine libraries display their holdings so it's easy to find what you're looking for, but a computer interface can also search the interior catalog for you.

BELOW The automatic, free book dispensers are common sightings at airports, subway stations and malls. OPPOSITE Shenzhen's citizens can check out free books 24 hours a day, 7 days a week.

2012. Several countries are incorporating vending machines into their public library systems, admiring China's programme.

SSIT's library machines are behemoths compared to their drinks-and-snack dispensing cousins. From a distance, the heavy, blue-and-grey boxes appear more like a bus stop to an oddly bureaucratic fantasy realm, rather than a repository of free books.

In the early beta versions of the machines, a reader would approach and peruse through long panes of glass displaying 400 books, each in its own narrow chamber and own corresponding ID. Alternately, you could attempt to interact with the catalogue interface built into the machine. This involved typing your query into a physical keyboard composed of steely, stiff keys. There was a notable time delay between pressing a key and seeing the character appear on the screen, which many library customers chose to fill with a string of vocalized obscenities. However, eventually, you could see if the library had your title, press a button or two, and watch a book drop.

Today, many vending machine libraries have been updated with QR codes, to make this process easier. It's the librarians who do the most adapting, their jobs more closely resembling mail carriers than bespectacled bibliophiles. Each day, they make their rounds to the machines, stocking each with new books and loading plastic bins of returned books into their van for re-cataloguing.

BELOW The Lonely Library was built to connect holiday-goers in Beidaihe with the serenity of the sea itself.

THE LONELY LIBRARY

QINHUANGDAO, CHINA

HOW TO FIND IT

From Qinhuangdao City, head south to the Ananya area of Beidaihe District. It's hard to miss if you look towards the sea. The library has no website, but to make an appointment, download the Anaya area app and search for 'lonely library,' or contact "The Lonely Library" on WeChat and request an appointment directly.

Getting to the library requires a 30m (98ft) walk through the sand. There is a reservation system in place and no photography is allowed in the reading room. You simply have to experience it with your senses, in the moment.

Many libraries vie for such superlatives as 'oldest', 'prettiest' or 'largest'. Few, however, have fought for the title of 'loneliest'. The moniker belongs without much contest to the brutal, cloud-grey building sitting on the seashore in Beidaihe, a resort area on China's Yellow Sea. It's hard to miss if you're trying to find it — from most angles, it's the only building in sight. The bare concrete, earth tones and sloping edges of the building make it seem like something plucked out of a *Star Wars* planet and dropped onto Earth by mistake. The library goes by many names, including the 'Seashore Library', or many people's simple favourite, the 'Lonely Library'.

The goal of Vector Architects, the firm who spearheaded the project in 2014, was to create a structure on the beach that mimicked the serenity of the sea itself; a 465 sq-metre (5000 sq-ft) work of art, forever staring back at its inspirational mother.

Dong Gong was the lead architect on the job. He thought about what kind of library should be built in the Beidaihe district of Qinhuangdao, a seaside region that many flock to as a haven — a vacation pause from daily life, an escape. Water-skiers, luxury yachts and bungee adventurers play along the shoreline. However, this is not everyone's idea of a holiday. One day, while Gong was brainstorming, he happened to glance at a painting by American realist Andrew Wyeth, depicting an old fisherman seated on a beach boulder, staring pensively at the

waves. The painting evokes profound loneliness, but also the exquisite connection with nature that can result from such depths of solitude. It was this feeling that Gong sought to infuse into the new library. Humans may not be able to survive underwater, but we can visit a terrestrial building designed to put us in sync with the ocean's natural rhythms.

The building's entire eastern wall is made of windows and doors, framing the full splendour of the sea. The goal was that everyone who enters the library can have an unobstructed view of the force of the ocean from wherever they are sitting. According to Gong, the main reading room is "an auditorium and the sea is the ongoing play." Sunlight filters in through the skylights and windows, and salty air weaves and wafts through the carefully placed vents.

Shelves upon shelves of books line the interior of the library, over 10,000 titles in total. But the massive, lonely building offers even more to those who make the journey to see it. There is a reading area, a meditation space, an auditorium, a cafe and a lounge. "According to each space, we establish a distinctive relationship between space and the ocean; define how light and wind enters into each room," said Gong. Although designed for introspection, the library regularly hosts poetry readings, dance recitals, plays, and chamber music concerts. When it was first built, it was the only building in sight for miles. Since then, Beidaihe has evolved into the beach town it was designed to be. Apartments and restaurants can now be seen in the background of the library if you stand at the right angle. Inside, however, nothing has changed. If you happen to visit, the architects hope you will feel what they intended: "When walking into the space, one starts to feel the light, breezes, and sound of the ocean. What comes after the perception is the unique spiritual linkage between each individual and the sea. In here, everyone can slow down the usual pace, and unfold the feeling of distance and loneliness different from the city life."

BELOW Many of the monastery texts are nearly a millennium old and only 20% have been scanned. **OPPOSITE** Visitors are welcome to explore the temple grounds.

SAKYA MONASTERY LIBRARY

TIBET AUTONOMOUS REGION, CHINA

The Sakya Monastery is a vast fortress of crimson roofs, imposing stone towers, and Buddhist endurance, sitting at over 4267 metres (14,000ft) above sea level, along the stark plateau of southern Tibet. The word 'Sakya' – which refers to the school of Buddhism seated at the monastery – translates to 'pale earth', in homage to the austere Ponpori hills that surround the complex.

Founded in 1073, the buildings that are present on the ground today are a melange of what has survived thousand years of conquerors, natural disasters, and the relentless passing of time. Following the 1959 Tibetan uprising and during Mao Zedong's Cultural Revolution, thousands of Tibetan monks were either executed or expelled. Buddhist art and manuscripts were deliberately burned, and many Tibetan temples were destroyed to pave the path for cultural progress. Hundreds of Sakya monks were sent into exile. Namkhai Norbu, a professor of Tibetan and Mongolian language and literature at Naples Eastern University, stated that only 36 Sakya devotees remained – along with, miraculously, their library.

The library at Sakya remains the largest surviving collection of Tibetan documents and artefacts anywhere in the world. Rumour has it that it was

"There is another, smaller room, illuminated
only by piercing rays of sunlight and the solemn glow
of a few butter lamps. Here is the precious library
that has survived a millennium."

preserved at the behest of Premier Zhou Enlai, a top official in Mao's cultural revolution campaigns, although history is not clear on what moved him to take this position.

Today, visitors can walk through the titanic entrance of Lhakhang Chenmo, the oldest surviving building at the monastery, built in 1268. Then, pass through a shaded hallway where copper prayer wheels glint in distant candlelight, and enter the immense court of the main prayer hall. The temple's soundtrack fills the air, a three-part harmony of chanting monks, curious tourists, and fluttering bird wings. Every so often, the low croon of a conch shell punctuates the noise. Behind the assembly hall's festival of prayer flags, bronze statues and red columns, there is another, smaller room, illuminated only by piercing rays of sunlight and the solemn glow of a few butter lamps. Here is the precious library that has survived a millennium.

The books are held in one continuous wall, nearly 61 metres (200 ft) in length, and a staggering 11 metres (36 ft) in height. According to legend, the wall holding the books was built so that even if the entire monastery were to collapse, its contents would remain standing. Currently, it supports hundreds of thousands of texts (the exact number seems to be debated) handwritten in Tibetan, Sanskrit, Chinese and Mongolian. The majority are canonical works of Buddhism, but there are many ancient works covering everything from history and philosophy, to poetry, astronomy, and even operas. Some are written on plant leaves. Some are written in gold ink. Some are bound in iron. One is a tablet of stone, clocking in at 500kg (1100 lb) – the heaviest book in recorded history. Art treasures abound, including a vast mural depicting the historical meeting between the Mongol Emperor Kublai Khan, and his guru, the Sakya monk Drogön Chögyal Phagpa, who would be the means that would convert the entire Mongolian empire to Tibetan Buddhism.

In 2011, monks and historians began a joint effort to digitize the contents of the library, but the work has been slow, and poorly funded. Currently, according to China News Network, only 20% of the library has been scanned, leaving much of its contents still shrouded in mystery to outsiders.

OPPOSITE Monks chant regularly in the main prayer hall of the Sakya Monastery, next to the library.

BELOW The stacks of the underground library go on and on. The library is always welcome to the public, both as a refuge from the heat and to inspire learning.

BHADARIYA TEMPLE UNDERGROUND LIBRARY

HOW TO FIND IT

3HX4+CR3, Fanta, Jaisalmer - Jodhpur Rd, Hwy, Bhadariya, Rajasthan 345031, India
+91 141 220 9860

There is a museum dedicated to the life of Bhadariya Maharaj, right next to the temple.

RAJASTHAN, INDIA

When he was a young man, Harbansh Singh Nirmal left his home in Punjab, and embarked upon the life of a sadhu, wandering the Himalayas, collecting wisdom and stories. One day, as he was trudging along a desolate road in Rajasthan, he came to a sudden realization: it was time to stop. A bus driver gave him a lift, dropping him off at a quiet, tumbledown village called Bhadariya. He took up residence in the town's dilapidated temple. As time went on, he asked the locals if they were interested in repairing the sacred structure. They agreed — on the condition that Nirmal supervised the work himself. So, he set to work.

An Orthodox Sikh preacher earlier in life, Nirmal would later describe himself simply as a 'believer in humanity.' The stocky, saffron-clad mystic drove around in a jeep and espoused animal rights, environmental justice, and the power of the Internet to bring people together. He began to plant hundreds of trees around the village and in the surrounding lands: pomegranates, date palms, wild cherry,

acacia and sacred *khejri*. He began a rainwater conservation project. The grounds of the Shri Bhadriyaji temple were revived with a 100-room rest house for spiritual pilgrims. Behind the whitewashed walls, Nirmal oversaw the completion of massive *Gaushala* – a protective shelter for stray cows – many of which had been abandoned or were at high risk of being smuggled into Pakistan and slaughtered. Today, the Gaushala's population ranges from a reported 5000 to 45,000 rescued cows.

The temple is officially dedicated to the goddess Bhadriya Mata, built by medieval warrior Maharawal Rawal Gaj Singh of Jaisalmer after he was victorious in a battle. However, according to some devotees, knowledge is said to be the biggest goddess of them all. Thus, the funds for renovating the temple were put to use building a temple of knowledge.

This was Nirmal's most ambitious act, perhaps: a library of over 9000 books, stored 4.8 metres (16 ft) beneath the temple. Initially, most of the books belonged to Nirmal, collected from his travels or simply given as gifts when pilgrims stopped by the holy grounds. Nirmal intended for the library to be a public sanctuary, a cooling, underground shelter from the searing heat of the Thar Desert. This literary cave of wonders can accommodate nearly 4000 people, who are welcome to read any book they wish at any time.

The books are mostly (although not exclusively) written in Hindi and Sanskrit, covering everything from mythology, astronomy, astrology and history, along with a healthy collection of epics and holy scriptures, as well as dictionaries and atlases.

Many villagers still reflect on Nirmal's apparent powers. A visiting businessman from Bhiwandi claimed Nirmal's touch corrected the misalignment in his fractured arm. A former government employee claimed he had the power to call ghosts and lost souls. Nirmal simply smiled at these comments. "I wouldn't call myself a miracle man," he said to reporter Rohit

"This literary cave of wonders can accommodate nearly 4000 people, who are welcome to read any book they wish at any time."

Parihar in 1999. Nevertheless, he is often credited as bringing the ghost town of Bhadariya back to life.

Nirmal eventually became known as Bhadariya Maharaj – a saint. He passed away in 2020. The temple, as well as the vast underground book sanctuary, is now taken care of by the devotees who live there.

LEFT Legends and holy texts from various faiths line the shelves. **BELOW** The warm streets of Jaisalmer, Rajasthan.

BELOW The library glows in the heart of
Levinsky Park every evening, beckoning
people to explore the shelves.

LEVINSKY GARDEN LIBRARY

TEL AVIV, ISRAEL

HOW TO FIND IT

Levinsky St 95 66052
Tel Aviv, Israel
thegardenlibrary.com

The Levsinky Garden
library and school
are primarily run
by volunteers in
Tel Aviv. There are
plenty of volunteer
opportunities,
including tutoring,
teaching arts and
crafts and even
organizing soccer
matches.

Just next door to Tel Aviv's central bus terminal lies Levinsky Park, a public space with a less than stellar reputation. Known for its frequent incidents of petty theft and drug deals, over the years it has also become a police drop-off point for undocumented immigrants and refugees. If they have nowhere else to go, it's where they sleep. *Roads and Kingdoms* have called it "A Park for Those Who Have Nothing."

If you visit Levinsky Garden at night, however, you'll notice a giant bookcase at its heart, radiating light.

The bookcase was founded (and remains maintained) by ARTEAM, an interdisciplinary art nonprofit, in collaboration with Mesila, a Tel Aviv aid centre for nonnationals. They typically refer to it as The Garden Library. In 2009, Yoav Meiri Architects constructed the library on the belief that access to a book is not a privilege, but a fundamental human right, offering both a means of escape and a haven from life's daily misfortunes.

"It was important for us that the library come to the people," a representative from Yoav Meiri Architects told *Arch Daily* magazine in 2011. "That those who maintain illegal immigrant status will come without fear, that the library would not have a closed door or a guard at the entrance who would check and ask questions."

The library is essentially two long bookcases. The first is taller and contains books for adults, with two large doors that open out to form a canopy, protecting

both the texts and their visitors from sun and rain. The shelves are illuminated from within so that, at night, the books appear to be glowing in the park, like a beacon. Across from the adult books is a shorter bookcase, welcoming children. The doors fold open into a clean floor, inviting you to stay a while and enjoy a story.

The library seeks to serve the park's community of immigrants, stocking approximately 3500 books in Mandarin Chinese, Arabic, Hebrew and English.

During the first three years, the librarians employed an innovative organization scheme. The books were not catalogued by genre or alphabetized by author. Instead, whoever picked up the book last was asked to re-shelve it based on how they felt after finishing. Categories included amusing, boring, bizarre, depressing, exciting, inspiring, or sentimental. A volunteer librarian would then enter the ratings into a database, adding it to the history of responses, which were noted on the spine of each book.

"The books wander between the shelves as their readers have wandered/are wandering the world," said the architects. "They carry with them their emotional history."

Initially conceived solely as a resource for Tel Aviv's migrant communities, the library rapidly evolved into an important community centre and meeting place for both the foreign and Israeli residents of the neighbourhood. Over time, the park has become a focal point for human rights protests. Sudanese and Eritrean refugees connect over shared struggles and assist each other in finding work and housing. A school offers language classes in Hebrew, French and English, as well as technical skills like programming and photoshop. But if you pass by at night, you can still see the bookcase that started it all, glowing bright, deep in the heart of the park.

KURKKU FIELDS' UNDERGROUND LIBRARY

KISARAZU, JAPAN

HOW TO FIND IT

2503 Yana, Kisarazu, Chiba 292-0812, Japan
+81 438 53 8776;
kurkkufields.jp

Guests staying overnight at Kurkku Fields can visit the library in the moonlight, after its public closing time.

When you enter Kurkku Fields in Chiba, you may feel as though you have stumbled into a fantasy realm. Vast green meadows and organic vegetable gardens stretch as far as the eye can see. Campers cook laid-that-morning eggs in cast iron frying pans set over woodfires, smiling children offer handfuls of snacks to baby lambs, and curious art sculptures — some resembling gigantic lava lamp drippings, or house-sized mirror boxes — peek over hilltops. It's the kind of place you want to fall into headfirst, hoping the magic will swallow you up. Which is exactly how the farm's library aims to make you feel.

Kurkku Fields' underground library is a design darling, built by Hiroshi Nakamura and NAP Architects, and camouflaged against the surrounding meadow of grass. Most people stumble accidentally into the entrance while wandering around. The front door ushers you down into the earth, to a sunlit cavern where softly domed walls are adorned with books. Plush chairs punctuate rolling hallways of texts, and the round, swirling ceiling opens at its pinnacle to allow beams of sunlight to shine through. In keeping with Kurkku's commitment to environmentally conscious design, the floor, walls, and ceiling of the library are planted with soil. Grass and

OPPOSITE The Kurkku Fields' library was designed to blend into the earth, as if it was born there organically.

moss installations grow from the edges, and caretakers can adjust between irrigation and water retention depending on the season. Soft, rectangular lanterns are installed periodically along the shelves, giving the impression that some of the books are made from solid light. Halls make meandering routes through the cavern, occasionally unveiling hidden reading rooms where unexpected volumes await discovery by curious patrons.

The land on which the library was built was originally a dumping site for construction debris, where nothing was growing. "We aimed to restore the lush valley that leads to the pond that farmers called Mother Pond," reflects a statement on Nakamura's website. "We believed that the architecture should not occupy the cultivated soil layer, but rather exist humbly under the flourishing of plants and micro-organisms in the soil. The earth has been regarded as the source of all life and a symbol of motherhood. Our wish was to make a small cleft in the earth, and create a tranquil place suitable for farmers to rest."

The library opened in 2023, with 3000 books waiting patiently to be found by whoever made the journey underground. Their topics mostly cover nature and agricultural techniques, but also poetry, history, religion, science, economics and philosophy.

Journalist Matthew Burgos summed up the sensation of the library in a 2023 article in *Designboom*: "Just as plants and vegetables grow with microbes in the soil as nutrients, people burrow into the ground to read books, accumulate knowledge, cultivate the power of imagination, and step on the earth again to move forward into the future."

BELOW Nanie Gunlao has been running
Reading Club 2000 out of his home in Manila
for over 20 years.

READING CLUB 2000

MANILA, PHILIPPINES

HOW TO FIND IT

1454 Balagtas St, Makati, 1204 Metro Manila, Philippines +63 0977 617 0486; readingclub2000.com

The club is always looking for volunteers to donate and sort books. Don't be alarmed if Guanlao offers to put you to work.

If you have purchased (or been given) the book currently in your hands, it likely means you are a bibliophile. Which means, also, that perhaps you have, at one point in your life, looked around your house and thought, *Hm. It appears I have too many books.* This was the problem faced by Hernando Guanlao. He loved his books and had too many. Books overflowing from shelves, books stacked haphazardly in the garage, books teetering from dusty shelves in the front room – books that he couldn't get rid of, because they are books.

He could almost sense their forlorn attitudes, sitting in musty piles, feeling unloved. This was years before tidying expert Marie Kondo sparked a decluttering craze, but Guanlao understood the idea that if you love something but you don't have the space for it, you should send it on its way to someone else who might enjoy it. Thus, Guanlao founded Reading Club 2000, in the year (you guessed it) 2000 – a library that is none other than his home, where people can come, peruse, grab a book, and either return it, or not.

The idea of the library is something of a tribute to Guanlao's late parents, to whom he credits his love of reading and education. Over 20 years later, the library/home/book temple has over 1000 tomes. Guanlao accepts all donations without complaint or fuss, welcoming them like lost orphans needing temporary shelter on their way to their forever homes.

"If the books want to be read, they come here," Guanlao told *The Guardian* in 2012. "People can borrow, take home, bring back or keep, or they can share and

"People can borrow, take home, bring back
or keep, or they can share and pass on to another.
But basically they should just take, take!"

pass on to another. But basically they should just take, take!" He refers to the books as bars of gold, and insists it is better to hand them out, without exceptions.

The titles at Reading Club 2000 are not organized by the Dewey decimal system, but are snuggled together thoughtfully, kept out of the rain and the dust of the street as best as possible (Manila's rainy season has caused flooding, leading to occasional losses from mould. But Guanlao is not deterred). A visitor can stop by and pick up anything from last decade's bestseller to rare editions and recent launches. Customers have included everyone from nursing students, thrilled to find rare medical references they could not easily buy elsewhere, to government healthcare workers excited to get reliable information on nutrition and human development.

In time, Guanlao realized he had a captive audience and decided to address them with his own philosophical, political, and spiritual ideas. "Why are we here?" he wrote in one of his first leaflets, which he distributed to library patrons. "If the universe is an accident, we are accidents unless there is meaning to its existence. A man's worth should primarily be determined by the kind of ideas, values and character he has and not by the amount of his wealth and power. What is more important is the character of a person. For a rich person without a good character can only give what your body needs but he cannot give warmth to your heart, he cannot give peace to your mind, he cannot enrich your soul. It is the life that we live which really matters."

His leaflets have covered anti-colonialism, dislike of rules, and the cascading social effects of weak, bloviating leaders. Through reading, he believes, we can learn to domesticate creativity, and "increase the number of creative persons to the point of critical mass".

In 1994, the Filipino government passed an act pledging to create more reading centres across the country. However, there are still only 1630 public libraries for the country's 113 million people – far below the ideal prescribed by the law, according to the National Library of the Philippines. For most children, books remain a luxury item.

People were eager to help Guanlao with his mission to be the change he wished to see in his world, and donations flooded in. Nevertheless, as time went on, the books he was receiving began to outpace his ability to store them. Thus, out of Reading Club 2000 was born Special Habit to Achieve Respect and Empower Many Others, or SHARE MO. The goal: to carry the books to the lower income barrios around the Manila Metro area. His call for help was answered by his neighbours, who help distribute the books further out.

Guanlao's oft-repeated mantra is: "Give of yourself. Give not 'til it hurts, give 'til it feels good."

OPPOSITE Guanlao turns no book away, saying 'if the books want to be read, they come here.'

© Karl Aguilar

THE BEACH LIBRARY

ALBENA, BULGARIA

HOW TO FIND IT

The library is located on the beach in front of Hotel Kaliakra (9620 Albena, Bulgaria.) The library has no postal address or phone number, but it is kept alive by Albena Resort, which can be found at Albena.bg.

There are three libraries now on the beach in Albena, but the original is still in front of Hotel Kaliakra.

The Black Sea is the resting place for over 25 rivers, flowing from just as many countries. It has over 11 names, depending on which coastline you are viewing from, and its brackish waters are home to countless shipwrecks, myths and fairy tales. Some modern archaeologists argue it is the final resting place of the real Atlantis. The ancient Greeks believed it to be the entrance to the kingdom of the dead. The islands that bedeck the surface of the water are sanctuaries for unique fauna and flora that can be found hardly anywhere else on Earth. In short, it is a place of incredible stories, where cultures flow past and through each other.

Along the Bulgarian coast, Albena is a vacation town, a spritely mix of beach umbrellas, pool floaties and green forests, a stark contrast to the dark and foreboding reputation of the Black Sea along which it resides. Albena sought to capitalise on its myth-like reputation by creating a cache of international stories, resting right in the sand..

The Bulgarian name for the Albena beach library translates into English as 'bookcrossing,' that is, a kind of crossroads where people from across the world leave their stories and pick up ones they may have never heard before. Like much of Albena's surrounding architecture, it's simple, arguably brutalist. It is not florid or showy, but invitingly efficient and helpful. If you forgot your beach book, don't fret: the beach library has everything you need.

OPPOSITE The shelves of Albena's library await beachgoers looking for their next read.

BELOW The library's shelves are kept organized by a staff of beachside librarians.
OPPOSITE Albena's gorgeous beach has made it a dream vacation spot in Bulgaria.

German architect Herman Kompernas was hired to design the structure – a simple set of white wooden shelves, weather treated to withstand the many moods of the Black Sea's atmospheres. "We found a material that is very resistant to sun and water" said Kompernas to *Euronews* in 2013. "We chose a sort of pallet construction for under the library to make it very stable against the wind." The shelves rest right in the sand, staring out into the expanse of the ocean, awaiting whatever Albena's transient crowd of beachcombers might bring its way. The shelves were initially loaded with a mix of thrillers, adventures, memoirs, children's books, detective stories and romances. However, over time, the genres and languages have expanded, as visitors are encouraged to leave their own books behind as well. Currently, over 6000 books rest on the shelves in over 15 languages (maybe more, depending on who the sea has washed up that morning). Vinyl shields are dropped down over the shelves like curtains during the rainy season, to prevent damage to the books.

The library is tended by a small group of beach librarians, whose job it is to keep things organized. Like any library, they do encourage you to bring back your book after you've finished.

BELOW The Rapana's shelves were made of flexible, airy wood. **OPPOSITE** Varna is the scene of many timeless stories of the Black Sea.

THE RAPANA STREET LIBRARY

In Memoriam

VARNA, BULGARIA

The 4000-year-old city of Varna developed out of a Thracian fishing village. Today, it is Bulgaria's marine hub, a thriving summer capital overlooking the Black Sea. Originally called Odessus, it would find itself under the dominion of Macedonian, Roman, Ottoman, Russian, and finally, Bulgarian rule. Always remaining an important port for seafarers and fisherman, Varna endured as a colony that lived in harmony with the Black Sea.

Today the raiding boats of the past are long gone, and most foreigners are brought in by cruises (Varna is the only Bulgarian city with a port big enough for the massive ships). Most of Varna's locals are involved in the fishing industry, the Bulgarian Navy, or the marine and oceanography research institute. The city's identity remains defined by its relationship with the sea on its front doorstep.

With a heritage that stretches over five millennia, Varna plays host to venerable museums, archaeological wonders, and breath-taking historical libraries. However, despite all of this, residents noticed a problem: many of the kids and teens in Varna weren't reading. The young people's lives were entirely based

"People were constantly wandering in, captivated by the Rapana itself, compelled to stay and flip through the titles."

on consumption of digital content, and the popularity of books was decreasing.

The design firm Downtown Studio took some delight in trying to solve this problem by adding something new to the urban landscape: a library, as unique as Varna's history..

Instead of heavy, colonial architecture or cheap plasterboard with florescent lights, the architects wanted a design that was light and transportable – something that mimicked the beauty of the Black Sea lapping at the shore, or the swirling mystery of a nautilus. To create a building that had all the flawless mathematical beauty of a seashell, the architects employed parametric design techniques – where ratios of space can be given to an algorithm and easily manipulated so they do not compromise integrity. Since the library was going to be free, the building also needed to keep to a modest budget. The materials selected were light, portable pieces of wood. The architects tested over 20 variations, determining the best number of curved pieces that could come together to create a seashell big enough in which to house hundreds of books. Eventually, a 240-piece structure of airy wood was born: the Rapana, named for a local genus of sea snail.

Immediately, curious visitors began to tumble in. The building resembled the skeleton of a titanic seashell – an undulating tunnel, unravelling from a single focal point, bursting with stories. Beams of sunlight shot into the heart of the buildings from the open, latticed roof, and sea air billowed in to mingle with the scent of old books. The shelves held around 1500 titles, but you would have been hard pressed to ever see it full. People were constantly wandering in captivated by the Rapana itself, compelled to stay and flip through the titles, entering one side of the tunnel empty handed, and leaving with a new book in hand.

Like a seashell, however, the Rapana was fragile. It was closed the same winter it was built, to save it from the snow and ice that batters Varna's shores. There are rumors that it will return as a permanent structure, although, like searching for an intact seashell on the beach, no one is quite sure when it will appear.

OPPOSITE The library's giant shape is designed to mimic the local seashells of the genus *Rapana*.

BELOW The Teylers public museum can be viewed
from the private, second floor library.
OPPOSITE Haarlem is a city that has preserved
its 19th century charm.

TEYLERS MUSEUM LIBRARY

HOW TO FIND IT

*Spaarne 16, 2011 CH
Haarlem, Netherlands
+31 23 516 0960;
teylersmuseum.nl/en*

The museum has
a calendar of
lectures, and
tours are easily
booked on their
website.

HAARLEM, THE NETHERLANDS

In the Netherlands, the city of Haarlem has happily kept its aesthetics ensconced in the 1800s. Even modern boutiques are situated under stained glass facades and fast-food chains surve burgers over waxed mahogany counters. A historian's dream village is incomplete without a library, and Haarlem has a glorious one. However, most people walk right underneath it, unless they know where to look.

Haarlem's Teylers Museum is the oldest museum within the Netherlands, a temple of 18th and 19th-century curiosities and Dutch masters' paintings, with a few rooms dedicated to modern innovations (just to keep you grounded in case you began to worry that you had, in fact, travelled back in time).

What few people know about Teylers, however, is that beyond the cabinets of ancient coins, fist-sized precious gems, and collages of luxurious oil paintings, there is a library – one so vast, the public relations rep at Teylers referred to it in a 2015 interview with *Museologue* as "the internet of the 19th century."

The library is on the upper floor of the museum's *Ovale Zaal* (Oval Room). Ascend the staircase and you'll feel like you're in an elongated globe of mahogany bookshelves, amidst the scent of leather

and aged paper. The museum's grand skylights are the only source of illumination, just as it was in the 1800s (indeed, on days when the weather is cloudy, it can be difficult to make your way around the shelves). Over 125,000 volumes rest tidily in glass cabinets. Topics such as 'ichtyologie' and 'ornithologie' are declared above each case in prim handwriting. There is no other library in the Netherlands with such a collection spanning knowledge across botany, zoology and various Earth sciences.

The Teylers library was the hottest place to research the latest scientific developments until roughly the middle of the 20th century. After that time, its relevance began to wane, but its historic value became immediately apparent. Visitors can imagine it as a bygone Wikipedia for scholars and scientists of the 1800s.

The library is not, strictly speaking, a public portion of the museum. There are only two ways you can enter: the first is to submit a scholastic request for carrying out research that requires actual use of the historical source material stored in the library. The second is to book an official tour, where a library employee can usher you through the precious rooms and will allow you to examine some of the books.

BETHNAL GREEN UNDERGROUND LIBRARY

In Memoriam

LONDON, ENGLAND

HOW TO FIND IT

Cambridge Heath Rd, Bethnal Green, London E2 0HL, United Kingdom +44 20 7364 3493; ideastore.co.uk/visit-us/bethnal-green-library

The Bethnal Green Underground Library was eventually turned into the subway station it was originally intended to be, but the above ground library was rebuilt and now welcomes visitors.

During World War II, a number of European librarians understood what bombs raining indiscriminately from the sky meant for their storehouses of books. With social services stretched thin, many took it upon themselves to smuggle their charges away into underground chambers and secret bomb shelters, in the hope that they would survive to the next chapter of history.

On 7 September 1940, a Nazi bomb exploded through the roof of London's Bethnal Green Central Library. The tidy book depository became a scene of destruction. Librarian George F. Vale and his assistant, Stanley Snaith waded through the rubble, trying to come up with a plan to salvage what remained.

Nearby, the half-finished Bethnal Green subway station had been transformed into a bomb shelter, providing refuge for over 5000 East Enders from the blitzing planes overhead. Snaith and Vale gathered the 4000 surviving books from what remained of the above-ground Bethnal Green library and descended into the cavern.

OPPOSITE The Bethnal Green subway station became a bunker during WWII, providing shelter for some 5000 people while bombs dropped from the sky.

"It is, perhaps, the least pretentious branch library yet built," said Snaith to the magazine *Library Review* in 1942. "Fifteen feet square, it is mere sentry box of a place... Libraries in converted shops, in village halls, in mobile vans, are common enough. But libraries in Tube shelters are something new under the sun."

To be fair, calling Bethnal Green a mere bomb shelter at that time is an understatement. It was essentially an underground village. In addition to rows of metal bunks, a 300-seat theatre had been built over the boarded-up train tracks, hosting operas, concerts, ballets and even weddings. A volunteer-led cafe served up hot pasties and sandwiches, and a medical centre offered basic healthcare. During a particularly vicious bombing raid, over 7000 people took shelter in its depths.

The underground Bethnal Green library was a shadow of its former, above-ground glory, but all the mightier for it. When the air sirens let out their mournful howl, and the bombs began to drop, the doors to the shelter were locked. In the necessary quiet, the theatre did not play a show, and the cafe did not fry bacon. But a book could still be cracked open, to take readers away from the horrors above.

"Each dusk sees the first contingent making its way down to the bowels of the earth," wrote Stanley. "The well and the ill, the old and the young, they come trooping down. Here a chokered docker, there an undersized lad with an Atlas load improbably poised on his head, playing prieux chevalier to a crippled mother. In the library, the youngsters are vocally busy with their book-selection, but why should they not chatter to their hearts' content?"

Patsy Crawley, a London resident now in her 80s, spent the first years of her life down in the Bethnal Green shelter. "It was a sanctuary to me," she said in a 2022 interview on *Historia* with author Kate Thompson, who wrote the novel *The Little Wartime Library* based on the Bethnal Green station. "By 1943, I was 14 and there had been so much horror...You can't

"The underground Bethnal Green library was a shadow of its former, above-ground glory, but all the mightier for it."

imagine what that library represented to me as a place of safety. It sparked a lifelong love of reading."

After the war, Bethnal Green was relieved of its duty as bomb shelter and was renovated into the subway station it was originally intended to be. The underground library was destroyed. However, the original above ground Bethnal Green library was rebuilt, and is open today, a reminder of the power of books to bring us resistance, entertainment, education and endurance during times of extreme hardship.

LEFT London endured incredible damage during WWII. **BELOW** Mr J. Mckinnon (Chief Assistant Librarian) supervises work in the underground shelter library in the early 1940s.

ST BRIDE FOUNDATION LIBRARY

LONDON, ENGLAND

HOW TO FIND IT

14 Bride Lane, London, EC4Y 8EQ
+44 20 7353 333;
sbf.org.uk/library

The library is free to access, but typically only by appointment. You may email the staff to request a time at library@ sbf.org.uk.

St Bride is known to many historians as the Catholic transmutation of Brigid – the Celtic goddess of healers, farmers, smiths, fertility and, perhaps above all, storytellers. St Bride's church on London's Fleet Street is a 17th-century architectural gem, whose tiered steeple is said to have inspired the traditional Western bride's wedding cake shape. Underneath the gleaming checkered floors and pews of the church's main hall, however, is a museum of ancient artifacts uncovered after the church's bombing in WWII. In the very back of this museum, past the glass cases of ancient Roman coins and gritty photographs of Nazi destruction, is a large stone well. In this spot, it is rumoured that thousands of years ago, the ancient pagans of Britain paid homage to Brigid, far before she became St Bride.

The caretakers keep a small candle lit in the mouth of this dark well, to honour the memory of the goddess-saint and all she represents. Perhaps it is no coincidence then, that Fleet Street became Britain's epicentre of storytelling well into the 20th century.

OPPOSITE The St Bride Institute is a gorgeous remnant of the bygone days of Fleet Street's journalism heydey.

"Today, the St Bride Foundation Library is
a charity, funding itself with tours and talks by
famous authors, publishers and bookmakers."

If you walked down the narrow alleys and lanes of Fleet Street in Victorian-era London, you would hear a cacophony of bibliophilia, the air alive with the clanging and clattering of printing presses. Wynken de Worde and Richard Pynson set up some of Europe's first printers here in 1500, and the neighbourhood would grow to house the publishing rooms for London's top international papers and countless penny presses. Fleet Street birthed the unions National Graphical Association and the Society of Graphical and Allied Trades. This was the heartbeat of the daily news.

In the late 20th century, record numbers of publishers exited Fleet Street with the advent of digital news, along with a reduction in government support for collective bargaining. A few remain, but one of the best hidden gems is perhaps the St Bride's Foundation Library.

Walk down Fleet Street today, past the commuter horns and petrol fumes of the main road, down into the quiet recesses of Bride Lane, behind the ancient worship site for St Bride, and you'll find the red brick building that house's St Bride Foundation Library – Britain's monument to journalism.

The library was conceived in 1891 by the St Bride Foundation, who took it upon themselves to preserve the extensive personal library of the late William Blades (a highly regarded printmaker). As time went on, the foundation became the final resting place for the personal book collections of numerous famous journalists and printing tycoons, along with presses, type-casting equipment, newspapers and other artefacts from across the history of modern printing. Some artefacts are locked away from the public and can only be read in the presence of a St Bride Foundation librarian, such as an extraordinarily rare copy of William Morris's *Kelmscott Chaucer* bound in white pig skin, or a copy of *The Consolation of Philosophy* by Boethius, printed in 1478.

In its heyday, the St Bride Foundation was an active school, where students of printing would come to learn how to work presses, refine their skills, and learn the latest technologies. The library was a living, breathing research station. Eventually, the school grew too large for the little brick building, and moved on to a larger campus, eventually becoming the London College of Communication.

Today, The St Bride Foundation Library is a charity, funding itself with tours and talks by famous authors, publishers and bookmakers. Many of the tours are guided by former workers of the printing trade, experts in their field.

Despite its prominence in London's history, the library of rare books and printing artefacts remains overlooked by most tourists, eclipsed by the grand church next door. But those who keep their eyes open will be pleasantly rewarded to find this hidden gem that encapsulates the history of London's Fleet Street.

OPPOSITE The St Bride Institute is a former communications school that now contains one of the largest collections of early printing press equipment in Europe.

BELOW The iconic red of K6 telephone booths
was initially disliked by most Englanders.
OPPOSITE The booths became so beloved that
when payphones became obsolete, some were
turned into libraries.

PHONE BOOTH LIBRARY

WESTBURY-SUB-MENDIP, ENGLAND

HOW TO FIND IT

At the corner of Top Road and Free Hill in Westbury-sub-Mendip, Somerset, England. westburysubmendip-pc. gov.uk/westbury-book-exchange/

There is a free, user generated Google map of all the known phone booth library sites in the UK, at bit.ly/ UKphoneboxlibraries

There are few symbols more iconic to the United Kingdom than the red telephone box. The original version, known as The K2, was designed in 1926 by Sir Giles Gilbert Scott and made entirely of wood. After the boxes were distributed to the public, its eye-catching red paint was met with frowns. Residents submitted complaints and repeatedly requested a less boisterous shade. It appears they were ignored.

The phone booth went through several iterations over the decades of the 20th century (including the ill-fated K4 unit, which dared to offer post office services in addition to a public telephone). But the one thing that remained consistent was the loud, red paint. It was the cast-iron K6 model, also designed by Scott, that became the iconic symbol of British charm that we know today. Over 60,000 units were installed.

In the early 2000s, the need for payphones was plummeting as mobile phone use skyrocketed. What was to be done with the K6 phone boxes, which had become so much more than a mere place to make a phone call?

The residents of Westbury-sub-Mendip came up with a solution. In 2009, the village lost access to their mobile library. When the government threatened to also take away their red K6 phone box, there was an official kerfuffle. Janet Fisher, a local resident, had an idea. At a tea party one day, she suggested that they

BELOW A view across the farmlands of the Mendip Hills in Somerset. **OPPOSITE** A patron explores what his local library has in store that day.

buy the telephone box from BT (British Telecom) and turn it into their own neighbourhood library. Parish councillor Bob Dolby and his wife installed four shelves and polished the box to a born-again shine. Residents donated their books, and someone posted a sign requesting "Silence please".

That same year British Telecom introduced a programme called Adopt a Phone Box. For a mere £1, you could buy the body of a classic K6 telephone booth and put it to work for absolutely anything – except, of course, to make phone calls.

Communities in the UK rushed to purchase the bold red boxes (the same ones once hated by their grandparents), and converted them into tea shops, art galleries, freecycle stands, and defibrillator access points. However, the majority have gone the way of Westbury-sub-Mendip and turned theirs into book depositories. Queen consort Camilla herself has been known to pop into the occasional booth and drop off mint-condition, signed copies of her favourite books for people to find.

Although the K6 box in Westbury-sub-Mendip was the first to be converted from phone booth to library, over 150 telephone booth libraries can now be found across the UK. Somerset has 14, Cambridgeshire has eight. There are two in Wales and one in Scotland, and there is even a K8 library in Clinton, New York (it seems one need not follow all BT's mandate for only converting K6 units if you live across the pond).

THE ARCADIAN LIBRARY

LONDON, ENGLAND

HOW TO FIND IT

Visiting the library is free, but the location is not available publicly. Vetted academics and tenacious bibliophiles with a sympathetic story may contact the library through their website: arcadianlibraryonline. com

In 2011, Alistair Hamilton published a book detailing the riches of the library itself: *The Arcadian Library: Western Appreciation of Arab and Islamic Civilization.*

Somewhere tucked inside the bustling labyrinth of London's streets, there is a clandestine library chronicling centuries of knowledge transfer between Western and Middle Eastern scholars. It seeks no publicity, has no signage, and permits no public images of its holdings or premises by outsiders.

The Arcadian Library, as it is known, is two rooms, watched over by lofty ceilings with walls of floor to ceiling books tucked neatly into pristine mahogany cabinets. Upon the shelves rest original medieval manuscripts, modern theses, first edition fairy tales, and a plethora of other vanishingly rare and ancient volumes. A custom emerald carpet, brightly embellished with a cornucopia of lilies-of the valley (the emblem of the library) graces the floor. In the main reading room hangs a panorama of medieval Cairo, crafted in Venice in 1549. The library is itself a temple of delicate symbols, an homage to Arabian and English artistry, a celebration of scholarship – and that's before you even open any of the books.

In a 2011 article for *The Times Literary Supplement*, librarian, author and historian Marina Warner described the experience of being in the library as introducing visitors "to a scholar-king's cabinet – to the palace of one of the cultivated Enlightenment rulers, for instance… the atmosphere is closer to a shrine, a grail chapel, and you feel, when you are there, usually alone with the books and the library staff, that you have been admitted by Lady Fortune to one of her favourites secret sanctums where wisdom is truly to be revealed."

One of the most curious details about the Arcadian Library is that its collector has chosen to remain completely anonymous. The secret, like the address

OPPOSITE London is home to the Aracadian Library, a private storehouse containing hundreds of years of knowledge exchange between the West and the Middle East.

of the library, is closely guarded amongst those few who have earned the right to know it. The more public faces of the library are Robert Jones, a rare book dealer, and Alastair Hamilton, esteemed scholar of modern and ancient Arab civilizations and languages. These two men are reported to have been the primary assistants of the nameless collector, helping them to amass what Warner calls, "one of the finest dedicated collections of books ever made about Western entanglement with the Middle East."

The library contains approximately 10,000 volumes, of which there are too many tantalizing choices to name in full. Some notable masterpieces include the original pamphlets from Ibn Sina (known also as Avicenna), the Muslim philosopher and father of early modern medicine in the medieval West. There is also a gold-laced, centuries-old edition of *The Arabian Nights*, printed on white vellum and illustrated in luxuriant colour by Edmund Dulac. There are medieval pilgrim's travel diaries, penned along their routes to Jerusalem and Mecca; accounts from traders who seem to be real-life versions of Sinbad the Sailor and Maruf the Cobbler; medieval papal indulgences concerning relations with the Ottoman Turks. There is also a forbiddingly precious copy of *Ibn Baklarish's Book of Simples* – a manuscript from 1130 which details remedies from Jewish, Christian, and Muslim heal-

ers in 12th-century Spain. The copy at the Arcadian Library currently holds the record for the earliest appearance of Latin script on paper.

The collection is a testament to a history of Western and Middle Eastern contact, but also bookmaking as its own art. "In this respect as well as in others," Warner reflected, "the library honours the tradition of the Middle East, where scriptural artefacts command special honour and shape aesthetics more generally: architecture becomes calligraphy,

"There are medieval pilgrim's travel diaries, penned along their routes to Jerusalem and Mecca; accounts from traders who seem to be real life versions of Sinbad the Sailor and Maruf the Cobbler."

clothing comprises documents, jewellery is inscribed with texts: the world aspires to the condition of a book, preferably finely bound."

The layered, rare beauty of the Arcadian Library is a once in a lifetime experience for any bibliophile. However, if you are content to view only its contents through your screen, its entire catalogue has been graciously digitized by its team of caretakers, so that scholars from around the world may benefit from its contents.

LEFT The exact location of the Arcadian Library is a closely guarded secret.
BELOW Photos of the library itself are forbidden, although its contents can be viewed online by scholars.

LES ARCHIVES NATIONALES

PARIS, FRANCE

HOW TO FIND IT

60 rue des Francs Bourgeois, Le Marais, 75003 Paris, France +33 1 40 27 60 96; francearchives.gouv.fr

Les Archives Nationale have an extensive digital catalogue, free for all to search. Current rules and process for visiting the archives in person can be found at francearchives. gouv.fr/en/ article/559150551.

Paris is an ancient city, whose spring gardens, patisserie-scented air, and cobblestone streets bely layers of underground secrets. One of the most overlooked is, perhaps, Les Archives Nationales at the Hôtel de Soubise. The exterior resembles a rather unassuming classical state building. Inside, however, is an opulent chateau that safeguards France's oldest and most precious books, locked away in mahogany shelves, only to be opened for the carefully vetted.

Even before it was one of France's most exclusive libraries, the chateau had a secretive past. The initial renovation was undertaken at the behest of King Louis XIV, who dubbed it Hôtel de Soubise, and gave it to his mistress, Anne de Rohan-Chabot, as her primary residence. The Hôtel's extravagant gilded accents, sumptuous furnishings and rococo flourishes are reminiscent of Versailles. Indeed, the décor is itself considered a part of Les Archives Nationales treasures – many trappings were collected from the homes of the aristocracy after the brutal revolution that toppled them.

The multi-building palace complex also contains a museum, Musée des Archives Nationales, which is open to all. The idea is to allow everyone to soak up these luxurious ornaments, once limited to the eyes of a select few. To the same tune, Les Archives Nationales is a proudly public library, declaring its contents free and open for the benefit of all French citizens. In other ways, the library more resembles a French version of the Vatican Apostolic Archives, containing the entirety of France's history, national treasures and secrets.

OPPOSITE Before the Hôtel du Soubise was home to restricted archives, it was home to King Louis XIV's mistress.

"Every room is filled floor to ceiling with dusty books and catalogues, each in their original crackled leather binding, and stuffed with thick handmade paper exhibiting characteristic uneven edges..."

The library hosts 373 km (232 miles) of physical records and 74.75 terabytes of electronic data. To handle this volume, it is technically split into different locations: documents from after the Revolution are stored in a building in Pierrefitte-sur-Seine, a suburb north of Paris. The portion that covers France's history up to and through the Revolution are held at the Hôtel du Soubise. This includes the archives of the churches of Paris and medieval city hall, as well as original records from France's Merovingian period, and from the reign of Charlemagne. Singular documents of note include *The Declaration of the Rights of Man and Citizen*, Napoleon's Last Will and Testament, and hand-penned letters from Voltaire, Marie Antoinette and Joan of Arc.

Some of these more famous documents are brought out for display in the museum and are circulated out every four months to protect them from UV damage. Because of their perilously delicate nature, permission to peruse the documents behind the public museum is possible to obtain but granted only to those willing to go through an extensive application process.

"Every room is filled floor to ceiling with dusty books and catalogues, each in their original crackled leather binding, and stuffed with thick handmade paper exhibiting characteristic uneven edges," said travel writer Noa Fineout, who had the privilege of visiting the stacks behind the museum in 2019.

The first few rooms contain records of expenses made by the royal family, many of whose bindings bear the name of Louis XIV's Minister of Finance Jean-Baptiste Colbert in etched gold. Some of these documents describe the life of these infamous royals in vivid detail. "I cracked open the King's most precious class of manuscript – Les Menus Plaisirs du Roi – in which the extravagant sensory experience accompanying each royal party is curated," remembered Noa. "I marveled over the minute scribblings that outline every sumptuous detail of the grand event, preoccupations that served as the definition of so many subjects' lives. It's impossible to absorb the incredible complexity contained within a single page and, even more, to recognise that the infinite knowledge replicated throughout the archives serves at the foundation for our presumptuous knowledge of this past – mere abbreviations of the multifaceted world kept alive in this building."

OPPOSITE The archives in this building contain texts from all of France's history through the Revolution.

BELOW The Magdeburg library also functions
as an outdoor reading room, concert venue
and community space.

THE MAGDEBURG OPEN-AIR LIBRARY

HOW TO FIND IT

At the intersection of Alt Salbke and Blumenburger Strasse, Magdeburg, Germany. The library is open 24 hours a day, and the residents are its librarians.

Concerts, readings and community events are often held at the library, organized by a wide variety of groups and businesses.

MAGDEBURG, GERMANY

Magdeburg is a city with a storied history. It was founded by Charlemagne in the 8th century, grew to be a promising stop on medieval trade routes, and fostered the early education of Reformation leader Martin Luther. However, in World War II Magdeburg was bombed by American and British forces, destroying most of the city centre and killing thousands. After the war, it was left to the Soviet Army, and what few baroque and medieval buildings that had survived the blitzes were destroyed. Behind the Iron Curtain, the city became a focal point for the machine industry. After German Reunification in 1991, many residents fled Magdeburg for the fresher-air fronts of West Germany. The Salbke neighbourhood was hit particularly hard, and quickly became characterized by unemployment, abandoned factories and brownfield land. A perfect place for a library.

In 2005, the tenacious residents of Magdeburg banded together to create the skeleton of a new book depository on the site of a previous library that had burned to the ground in the 1970s. For this, they chose something teasy to find: beer crates. Once the structure had been formed, a small two-day reading and poetry festival took place. Many residents came out to see what was going on. Suddenly, there was life on the old library's grave. Inspired, the residents decided to turn their open-air beer crate library into something permanent.

Professionals were brought in: architects working at Karo* design firm, led the project. A group of professional designers and architects took stock of what the residents wanted and needed and drew up several designs. The residents also began collecting used books from local homes, and from nearby towns. In total over 20,000 books were collected. To continue the upcycling theme, the designers chose to reuse tiles from a 1960s department store façade in Hamm. Funding from the Federal Government kicked in, and the library officially opened in 2009. The "beer crate library" as it had been fondly called up until that point became The Magdeburg Open-Air Library, eventually winning the European Prize for Urban Public Space.

With no doors to lock, anyone is free to peruse the shelves 24 hours a day. The librarians are the residents themselves. Reading gardens and nooks built into the wooden walls beckon readers to stay a while and enjoy the green space. The building also contains a stage where children's plays are performed, public readings are held, and small concerts are staged. Upstairs is a cafe. The books are shelved in glass cabinets built into the long wooden wall.

The library and its retro-futuristic design is embraced by the residents of Salbke, as a sign towards a brighter future from the postwar period.

THE HOME LIBRARY OF BRUNO SHRÖDER

HOW TO FIND IT

This library cannot be visited. It's real, but there is no publicly available address, no opening times and the librarian is deceased.

METTINGEN, GERMANY

If you consider yourself a bookworm then you may, at one point, have imagined what it would be like to own a fantasy library. The daydream might involve a vast room in a castle, perhaps with a floor of marble, and a maze of spiral staircases ascending cathedral-height walls, stacked from top to bottom with books. Or perhaps it is a dark cavern, accessed by secret passage and lit by torchlight and lamps, whose silence is punctured only by the rattling of iron keys, with endless aisles of books descending into the dark. These are the private libraries of princesses, monks and wizard-kings. But ordinary people cannot have fairy-tale libraries. Unless, of course, you are Bruno Shröder.

Shröder was a resident of Mettingen – a charming German countryside town of timber-framed homes, red-brick streets, and the occasional meadow of frolicking horses. A structural engineer by trade, when he wasn't at work he could

OPPOSITE Bruno Shröder turned his home into a wall-to-wall library. The combined weight of the books is estimated to weigh as much as 15 cars.

"In the attic, it seems,
frustrated at running out of wall space,
he began building into the ceiling."

often be caught perusing his local bookstores. He eventually retired from his day job, but his enjoyment of engineering work did not diminish. Neither, it seems, did his love of books. For lack of anything better to do, he turned these energies onto his own home. At least, this is what we assume happened. Shröder passed away before anyone could ask him what, exactly, was going on inside his house.

Video footage we have from the interior reveals a home library that seems straight out of a Roald Dahl book. Beginning in the foyer, nearly every wall is covered in row after row of solid books. In the attic, it seems, frustrated at running out of wall space, he began building into the ceiling. These are not haphazard stacks that were thrown together quickly – each section of the home library is meticulously organized, and poetry, fiction, guidebooks, textbooks, and nonfiction are all represented. The basement is coated from wall-to-wall in thrillers, and the works of Arno Schmidt, for whom we can only assume Shröder had a special fondness, are kept in glass cases.

One of the most satisfying aspects of a physical book is the weight of it against your palms – however, that weight, multiplied over nearly 80,000 volumes, can sum up to a force of destruction. According to the calculations of Guido Kleinhubbert, journalist at *Der Spiegel*, Shröder effectively added the weight of 15 cars to the frame of his house. And yet, the structural integrity is completely sound, absorbing the many thousands of tomes with grace. This is likely where Shröder's engineering background served him well. The custom shelves and carefully designed roof attachments were done with expert calculations. In short, the man knew exactly what he was doing (and the rest of us should be cautious before trying this in our own homes).

Apparently unsatisfied at a mere physical organization of his beloved books, Shröder was also in the process of creating a digital catalogue of his collection, complete with reviews, but he did not get the chance to finish.

Shröder passed away in June 2022 – with no notes in his will about what should happen to his books. His estate manager remains baffled as to what to do. Thankfully, no one involved seems to be able to bear the thought of throwing the books away. So, for now, they sit in Shröder's silent home – patiently waiting whatever comes next.

OPPOSITE Shröder was a structural engineer. He carefully calculated how to wallpaper his house in books so that the frame remained intact.

BELOW Antonio La Cava drives his three-wheeled book van up the narrow hills of Basilicata. It has often been dubbed Italy's smallest library.

THE BIBLIOMOTO-CARRO

BASILICATA, ITALY

HOW TO FIND IT

Being a mobile library, the Bibliomotocarro has no fixed address, but still makes regular rounds across Basilicata. You can find Antonio La Cava's latest route at maestrolacava@gmail.com.

In 2019, Antonio la Cava was named Commendatore dell'Ordine al Merito della Repubblica Italiana (Knight Commander of the Order of Merit of the Italian Republic) in recognition of his service to the children and culture of Italy. But he still prefers you call him Antonio.

Inside the arch of Italy's 'boot' is Basilicata, a province of stark proportions. Nearly half of the land is jagged mountains, into whose limestone peaks are carved ancient churches and prehistoric rock dwellings. Sun-bleached buildings clamber up peaks to form villages, as granite outcroppings overlook the Ionian Sea like stony gods.

Through the winding streets of Basilicata's most remote villages, you can occasionally hear the tiny chugs of a three-wheeled van: the Bibliomotocarro – Italy's smallest library. It looks itself like something that has fallen out of a children's book. The tiny truck – a Piaggio Ape, the three wheeled version of the vespa – is painted robin-egg blue and topped with a shingled, fairy-tale roof (complete with chimney). Inside, three long shelves of children's books line each side of the van.

The driver is Antonio la Cava, who, 20 years ago, transformed his Piaggio into a mobile library for the children of Basilicata's most isolated mountain communities. "I was strongly worried about growing old in a country of non-readers," la Cava told the BBC in 2019. "The Bibliomotocarro is a travelling library that brings books where they are needed without denying any child the right to have the book that he desires, directly in his hand."

When la Cava's cheerful blue van drives into one of these cloistered villages, children can often be seen trailing behind him, waiting for the moment the van stops so they can see what new books are in store for them. la Cava parks and opens the doors to the interior – painted like red bricks – and throws open the glass bookshelves so the children can begin to peruse. He never rushes them, but occasionally offers to read a story to a child who cannot manage on their own yet.

La Cava's work is supported by Fino ai Margini (Up to the Edge), a charity group which runs literacy and writing programmes in the smallest, remotest parts of Basilicata, where isolation is a major factor of daily life. Many of these villages have less than 1000 adults, and even fewer children. At one time, in San Paolo Albanese on the slopes of Mt Carnara, there were only 270 adults, and just two children. There was no school in the village, so la Cava would make a point to stop there every Sunday morning and ensure San Paolo Albanese's children– of which there were two – got whatever books they desired.

"Is it worth it?" is a question often put to la Cava, especially in the context of driving over 1000 km (621 miles) to deliver a handful of books to two children. "It's not only convenient, but it is right," he replies in a 2019 interview with BBC.

The Bibliomotocarro does more than hand out books, however. In one project, led by la Cava, children were invited to write the first chapter of a story. Then, he took the chapters to the next village, where he invited those children to write the second chapter of the same story, and so on. In this way, the Bibliomotocarro helps connect the isolated children of the high peaks of Basilicata, and ensures they never run out of stories to read, or to tell. The little blue van has inspired similar mobile libraries across Italy, such as the Ape Randagia in Concesio and the BiblioApe in Tuscany.

BELOW The illuminated compartments of the
Future Library contain manuscripts no one
is allowed to read until 2114. **OPPOSITE** The
Future Library is housed inside the Deichman
Bjørvika public library.

THE FUTURE LIBRARY

OSLO, NORWAY

There are public libraries, and there are private libraries. But has there ever been a library where no one – not even the librarians themselves – are allowed to read the books? Perhaps not until the Future Library 'opened' in 2014.

In a sense, the library has two locations. One is a scrappy patch of infant evergreen trees, nestled in the heart of the Nordmarka forest outside of Oslo. The other is on the top floor of Oslo's Deichman Bjørvika Public Library, in a small room that resembles something between an Egyptian tomb and a cocoon made of pale wood. "It's quite small," said Anne Beate, Chairperson of the Future Library Trust, who runs the library. "We ask everyone to take off their shoes before you enter. This is to help people get into the right mental mode, to show respect, to help you slow down. I've had people come in and start crying. I've had people not understand what they are looking at. Sometimes I meet youngsters in there hanging out doing their homework. Whoever you end up in there with, it often ends up being a shortcut to deep conversation. We call it the 'Silent Room' – but really it's a room for dialogue, a place where people see themselves reflected in each other's eyes, asking each other what 100 years means to them."

The walls of the Silent Room are built from thousands of thin, wooden tiles, their beige simplicity punctuated by 100 searing lines of light. These contain original manuscripts of unread, unpublished stories by the likes of famous authors such as Margaret Atwood, Ocean Vuong and Tsitsi Dangarembga. But all you can do is stare. These books are only for future beings.

Each year since its founding, the trust that runs the library has approached a high-profile author with an unusual prompt – to write a story that will be read by no one else. A modest ceremony marks the occasion of each story's arrival at the library – held amongst the young trees in the Nordmarka forest. Then, the library locks the unread manuscript away into one of the glowing glass shelves of the Silent Room. They have never been turned down by an author.

All stories are 'displayed' in the Silent Room in Oslo, only to be enjoyed after the year 2114, by whoever is around to read them. "Some people are happy, some people are provoked that they cannot read the books," Beate notes. "There is a Margaret Atwood story right there, you know? And we can't read it."

The 1000 trees that were planted in the Nordmarka forest at the inception of the library will eventually grow up to be the paper that these unread stories will be printed on, together in one anthology. The plan today is that 4000 copies of the anthology will be printed. There is no plan to print the anthology beyond the pulp that is available from the trees planted in Nordmarka. "But who knows what will happen. The trees could burn. Climate change could ruin the forest. The future trustees of the library will need to interpret the mandate we have left them, and may be asked to find solutions to a problem we can't even see," said Beate.

This is a bit of the point. The Future Library and Trust was created by Katie Paterson, a conceptual artist who focuses on connecting people with deep-time through such projects as a telephone line that connects users to a melting glacier and the creation of a map feauturing 27,000 dead stars. The Future Library is designed to collapse the view between our own lives, the environment, and the future. It is a face of bold optimism while honestly staring down the barrel of climate change; to Beate, it insists there will be books in the future.

"We learned a long time ago to let go of control," Beate continued, "to embrace a willingness to invest in something that is not for me. Or even for you. I think that is something the world needs. This is why we've set up a trust – and it's called a trust because our only option is to trust the coming generations

that they will care and look after this work for 100 years. Although, I often like to turn it the other way around, and think about it from the other side, too. This future generation, in fact, they have to trust us – that we cared for investing and starting these kinds of projects now. So that there is something for them to take over."

LEFT The futuristic Deichman Bjørvika library building invites contemplation of the future.
BELOW The entrance has no major descriptors. It takes people a moment to discover what they are looking at.

THE LONGYEARBYEN PUBLIC LIBRARY

SVALBARD, NORWAY

HOW TO FIND IT

SJ, Longyearbyen 9170, Svalbard (just off the main street, Hilmar Rekstens vei)
+47 79 02 23 70; lokalstyre.no

Although the librarian heads home in the late afternoon, the library remains open to members until 11.00pm, to help ease the passing of long winter nights.

If you travelled to the tip of Norway, then continued 804 km (500 miles) further north into the frigid dark of the Arctic, you would eventually come upon Svalbard. In this land of extremes, polar bears roam over windswept hills of ice. Puffins, terns and kittiwakes spread their wings in air temperatures that can freeze human breath in an instant. Tusked walruses and pale beluga whales plunge in and out of ink-black water, bedecked with star-white ice flows. In the long winter, the sun becomes a memory, and the land is ruled by night. Avalanches, mudslides and blizzards are the norm. The theme in Svalbard is resilience: those not tenacious enough to endure simply do not survive.

Initially, the promise of whale oil and coal tempted prospectors to brave the unforgiving climate, and the remnants of Victorian mining settlements and bygone science outposts still decorate the stark landscape today, some becoming the bones of modern research stations.

In terms of governance, Svalbard plays by its own rules. In 1920, the Spitsbergen treaty officially granted the archipelago under the protection of Norway, but citizens of all nations who signed the treaty have equal rights. The residents

OPPOSITE
Longyearbyen is the world's northernmost settlement, surrounded by Arctic tundra.

"If Svalbard had a capital, it would be Longyearbyen, a small mining town with nearly 2000 inhabitants, and the home of the world's northernmost cache of books: the Longyearbyen Public Library."

of Svalbard seem to understand that resilience is impossible without cooperation, and the assurance of mutual good.

If Svalbard had a capital, it would be Longyearbyen, a small mining town with nearly 2000 inhabitants, and the home of the world's northernmost cache of books: the Longyearbyen Public Library. But getting this many volumes into this unforgiving landscape was no easy feat.

In 1918, a week before 1 May (Norway's Labour Day), a group of coal miners asked their manager if they could have the day off, in order to purchase painting, banners and ingredients for baking cakes. On 1 May, the residents and workers of Longyearbyen banded together in a worker's strike. Their banners demanded an eight-hour work day, a children's school, bathing facilities and a public library. They were ignored. In 1919, the coal miner's union offered to contribute 500 crowns (50 times more than an average day's wage), for the creation of a library for the workers, if the managers would match their

donation. Eventually, the 'Statutes for the Workers library' was approved. The library was open three days a week, run by a head librarian and two assistants.

The fledgling book depository was beloved, but immediately beset by problems. The residents of Svalbard do not tend to stay long, and sourcing dedicated staff and reliable funds proved difficult. Then, WWII came to Svalbard's shores. Although the region sought to remain neutral, the entire town of Longyearben was bombed. Nearly all buildings were burned or reduced to rubble.

Once the dust had settled, the union had two clear goals: restart the insurance fund, and build a library as soon as possible. Two workers set about combing through the rubble, looking for what books survived. The Women's Society, the town priest, and the coal miners banded together to assert the creation of a more permanent, safely funded, and well-armoured structure to house the world's northernmost books. Eventually, in 1949, the Governor of Svalbard declared the Longyearbyen Public Library open. The new building was stocked with the remnants of the former coal miner's library and what remained of the town's modest church library.

Today, the library is well-stocked, warm, and serves as a symbol of resilience of the people of Svalbard. Although most residents are still transient (the average stay of a Svalbard citizen is under 5 years) a purple and white library card from the Longyearbyen Public Library is a token of proof that you journeyed to the northernmost human settlement on earth – and stopped to read a book there.

OPPOSITE The Longyearbyen Public Library only exists in its comfortable, well-funded state today because of decades of work by miners, scientists and union workers.

BELOW Ivan III's library may have never
existed, but many parts of the Kremlin have
also never been excavated, leaving many to
wonder.

THE LOST LIBRARY OF THE MOSCOW TSARS

In Memoriam

History's greatest civilizations are known for their exalted libraries. This includes the Library of Alexandria, a veritable university that housed half a million scrolls from India to Macedonia, or the Imperial Library of Constantinople, which was said to hold a millennium's worth of Greek and Roman knowledge. Although these brilliant temples of knowledge were, sadly, destroyed, most historians can agree that they did at least exist.

This is not the case for the Lost Library of the Tsars, also known as The Golden Library.

In 1462, Ivan III became the first tsar of Russia. Under his reign, he tripled the country's territories, renovated the Kremlin, and introduced a new legal code. According to legends, he also amassed a vast library of ancient scrolls and artefacts from the Atlantic to the Pacific, a treasure horde of unquantifiable historical value.

The trouble is, no one has ever been able to find it.

According to legend, Ivan III (also known as Ivan the Great) founded his great library in the 16ᵗʰ century, stocking it with books written in Greek, Latin, Chinese and Egyptian. Spoils from the ancient libraries of Constantinople and Alexandria were said to have found refuge there, along with the books that Byzantine Princess Sophia Palaiologina – Ivan III's third wife – brought with her to Russia as

"The implication is that the library could reveal to us important historical figures that have otherwise been lost to time."

part of her dowry. The library apparently disappeared under the reign of their grandson, Ivan the Terrible – a bellicose leader known for unpredictable bouts of rage.

Maximus the Great, who visited in Russia in 1518, detailed in his biography that during a visit to Russia he was shown a storeroom of ancient Greek books in the Kremlin – remarking that even in Greece itself, he had not seen their equal. A few centuries later, in 1724, a Russian officer wrote that he had discovered a secret passage in the Kremlin full of trunks, only to have his superior ban anyone from accessing the rooms. In 1819, a professor in Estonia found a document that lists specific titles and authors of books from a tsar's library – but neither the author of the list nor the tsar in question are named. The list describes 142 volumes of Titus Livius's *History of Rome* (historians are only aware of 35) along with an unnamed poem by Virgil. Most notably, the list contains author names that historians had simply never seen before – but were notable enough in their time to have apparently belonged in the personal library of a tsar. The implication is that the library could reveal to us important historical figures that have otherwise been lost to time. This has lit a fire under some historians, to figure out where the library – or at least its contents – are now.

OPPOSITE *Ivan the Terrible Showing His Treasures to Jerome Horsey by Alexander Litovchenko, 1875. Paintings like this keep alive the hope of finding the library, or at least its contents.*

Peter the Great and Napoleon were said to have sent expedition teams to the Kremlin, seeking out Ivan III's treasure trove of knowledge. In the early 1890s, Eduard Thraemer, a professor from the University of Strasbourg, journeyed to Moscow to begin a years-long search for evidence of the library, but was ultimately unsuccessful. In 1893 an eminent historian and archaeologist, Ivan Zabelin, published an article titled *The Underground Chambers of the Moscow Kremlin* where he argued Ivan III's library had existed underneath the Kremlin, but surely had been destroyed. In response, and spurred by the promise of a once-in-a-lifetime discovery, attempts at excavating underneath the Kremlin began. A series of underground chambers and tunnels were discovered, but none contained any books. The historian and author SA Belokurov became dedicated to finding the library, studying every source he could find. Eventually, he hit a wall, concluding that many of the stories that had been passed down must have been legends. Then in the early 20th century, archaeologist Ignatius Stelletksii discovered maps of the Kremlin from different centuries, including areas believed to be sealed off, and even negotiated permission from the Stalin government to excavate. However, the outbreak of World War II halted the work.

A handful of historians continue to peck away at the mystery, intent on finding this bibliophilic Atlantis, especially since many underground areas of the Kremlin have never been examined. One legend states that Ivan IV cursed the library, so that anyone coming close to its location would go blind.

The only thing that remains certain is the enigma, and the tantalizing possibility of discovering a library that could change our perception of history.

BELOW The cabin library blends seamlessly into the Eas Mor forest. OPPOSITE The Isle of Arran is believed by some to be the original site of Avalon.

THE LIBRARY
IN THE EAS
MOR WOODS

ISLE OF ARRAN, SCOTLAND

HOW TO FIND IT

Eas Mor is 1.6 km to 3 km (1-2 miles) from Kildonan in the south of Arran. There is a car park and a bus stop near the entrance just off the A841. easmor-ecology.com

```
A GPS route
through the
woods to library
can be found at
walkhighlands.
co.uk/arran/eas-
mor.shtml.
```

Floating in Scotland's Firth of Clyde, the Isle of Arran is a land of green hills, misty dells, whispering forests and crashing coasts. Some believe it is the site of the legendary Emain Ablach, a paradisiacal land of apples. Others call it the home of the shapeshifting sea god Manannán mac Lir. A few even consider it the original site of Avalon, the heavenly otherworld where King Arthur whiles away the afterlife.

Eas Mor is one of the many forested areas you can wander on Arran. Wide, welcoming paths lead through the dewy trees to a fairy tale-worthy waterfall. The brilliant stream descends into a pool 31 metres (103ft) below, known as the Hidden Valley. Most people know about the waterfall, but on the cliffs behind it, hidden away amongst the trees, there is also a library.

Reaching the library requires a steep walk a bit over a mile through the forest, with little signage or other landmarks to help guide you. You will know once you arrive, however, as it's the only building in sight.

The unassuming log cabin sits by itself in a glade, a single room of stacked logs with two windows and a roof carpeted in green moss. It is easy to imagine a modest hobbit stepping outside to greet you with a

wave and a cup of tea. Inside the library, you'll find yourself surrounded by paper – books of every variety, yes, but also notes left behind by visitors from across the world. Some are the happy drawings from children, excited to share tales of their day in the forest. Others are poems, inspirational quotes and well-meaning messages. Some are quiet letters to the dead. The missives are on walls, crowding the window frames and floating down from the ceiling, like clusters of pinned wings. The little room seems to be able to take no more. However, in the corner, there are stacked sheets of clean, fresh paper and a large basket of coloured pencils, so that new visitors can contribute to this tangible collection of thoughts and experiences. If a book speaks to you amidst the paper, you are encouraged to take it, and to leave one behind.

The library may appear to be managed by otherworldly attendants, but it is in fact kept organized by Eas Mor Ecology, a volunteer group whose goal is to transform the Eas Mor woodland back into its natural state after decades of commercial forestry. Their motto is 'man can never own the land, only manage it.' The group originally built the cabin from trees felled by a storm in 1998 and today helps keep the walking paths clear for whoever chooses to make the trek to the little library behind the waterfall.

THE VAN LIBRARIES OF THE HEBRIDES ISLANDS

STORNOWAY, SCOTLAND

The Hebrides are a chain of small, rugged islands reaching up across the western edge of Scotland, as if yearning for the Arctic Circle – home to pristine (if chilly) beaches, misty moors and wind-whipped hillsides, each with their own unique characteristics. The islands all contain one common attribute however: their incredible isolation. To describe the communities that live in the Hebrides as 'remote' is an understatement. Seventy-three percent of the population live in villages of less than 3000 residents and must drive at least one hour to reach a town that has at least 10,000 residents.

People born in these far-flung settlements often move away in search of greater job opportunities. A 2007 migration study showed the population had declined by over 40% between 1901 and 2001, with a negative birth rate. This establishes a cycle in which the already limited infrastructure experiences reduced demand, resulting in even fewer resources for those who remain. In most locations, public buses are available only once a week outside of school term. Rubbish collection occurs less than every two weeks. One service that has remained fully funded, however, is the library.

HOW TO FIND IT

The mobile library is always on the move, but the main branch is in Stornoway, the main town in the Hebrides, at 6 Kenneth Street, Stornoway, HS1 2DA Lionacleit Library +44 01870 603691, Stornoway Library +44 01851 822744; wilibraries.org.uk/ Mobile-Library

For patrons who are housebound or do not wish to browse the stock in the van, the driver-librarians will happily deliver pre-selected books to individuals' front doors. If a patron is not sure what they'd like to read, the librarians often make a point to get to know them and make recommendations based on their tastes.

OPPOSITE The Outer Hebrides library van travels for hours between rural villages, hand delivering books to remote residents.

Because of the vast distances between where residents live and their nearest library branch, the Western Isles Public Library of the Hebrides developed a mobile library programme. Currently working out of two vans – each painted with the Gaelic word *leabharlann* along with its English translation, "library" – librarians make regular rounds between remote neighbourhoods, delivering fresh books to rural schools, care homes, or even directly to private residences. The routes typically cover more than 800 miles of desolate roads and serve nearly 1000 residents.

The library's van service actually began operating decades ago, when most residents of the Hebrides were farmers, and cars were still a luxury. For people who couldn't afford to buy books or drive significant hours all the way to the library branch, the mobile library became their primary connection to the outside world.

In the 21st century, for some residents, it is still a lifeline to culture and humanity. The van service is especially helpful for disabled people for whom driving over an hour is extremely difficult. In an increasingly socially isolated, digital age, a visiting librarian might be the only human contact they receive on a regular basis.

These mobile libraries also offer something extremely precious to Scotland's dwindling population of native language speakers: books in Gaelic. The Hebrides contain Scotland's highest concentration of Gaelic speakers, but there are few books in this threatened language. They are also frequently not available on e-readers or are very expensive to purchase. The quantity of Gaelic books carried by the library allow readers to peruse based on their reading level and enjoy a richer breadth of stories.

Despite Scotland engaging in a slash and burn approach to library funding over the past decade (30 branches shuttered their doors in 2017), the mobile library in the Western Isles continues to stay well-funded by the local government. However, there are

"The Hebrides contain Scotland's highest concentration of Gaelic speakers, but there are few books in this threatened language."

concerns the mobile library is on its last legs, with vans in urgent need of repairs.

Some people have proposed substituting the mobile libraries with more online reading resources, but communities have pushed back, worried about losing access to the Gaelic language texts that the library provides. Also, more frequently, patrons say it's simply not the same as talking to the librarian, and many would grieve the loss of getting to hold a new, freshly picked book in their hands.

LEFT The Hebrides are home to pristine natural landscapes. **BELOW** The library makes a point to advertise itself in Gaelic as well as English.

BELOW Rossend Arús' library is tucked
away on Barcelona's streets, but he always
insisted it be available to the public.
OPPOSITE The original sign still hangs
above the library entrance.

ARÚS PUBLIC LIBRARY

BARCELONA, SPAIN

HOW TO FIND IT

Passeig de Sant Joan 26, 08010 Barcelona, Spain
+34 932 565 950;
bpa.es/es

The library contains a Sherlock Holmes collection of over 6000 books in 42 languages.
It also boasts one of the world's most comprehensive Sherlock Holmes collections.

The Arús Public Library is not a library that its founder Rossend Arús intended to be difficult for the average citizen to find. However, amidst Barcelona's colourful alleys, grandiose architecture and other bright distractions, many people find themselves walking past it, even if they are deliberately looking for it.

The library is tucked away on the second floor of a 19th-century townhouse, whose beige facade suggests nothing of great import is to be found inside. An ornate lantern is the only giveaway, illuminating a small stained-glass sign that reads Biblioteca Pública Arús. Enter the hushed building, climb up the marble staircase, and visitors will be rewarded with an arresting sight: an indoor replica of the Statue of Liberty, known as the Catalan Liberty. She bears the words 'Anima Libertas,' Latin for 'Freedom of the Soul.' These simple words summarize the library founder's belief that every man, whether rich or poor, can achieve intellectual liberation through education. At the base of the statue are a series of tiles that read, 'Salve' – Latin for 'Welcome'.

Accept the Catalan Liberty's greeting, walk a few steps beyond her entryway, and you will find yourself in a library fit for a Spanish prince. Globe lanterns, bronze statues and gilded floral reliefs illuminate

BELOW The Catalan Liberty greets library patrons at the top of the steps. **OPPOSITE** The library is stocked with hundreds of titles on Freemasory, which often led to scandal.

over 80,000 books, and sumptuous mahogany tables beckon a session of study.

The library was once the private collection of Rossend Arús, a playwright, journalist and outspoken believer in the education of the working classes of his beloved Catalonia. He left clear instructions for how his fortune and home should be dealt with upon his death, and in 1891 (four years after his passing), the Biblioteca Pública Arús was officially opened.

Arús was a prolific member of the Freemasons, and his library contained, among other things, hundreds of books on the philosophies and history of Freemasonry – a collection that would come to haunt its future.

In the 1930s, the Spanish Civil war brough Barcelona to its knees, and Catalonia fell under the control of dictator Francisco Franco. Backed by the Catholic Church, Franco began a campaign of hate against all enemies of the ministry. This included labour unions, communists, Jews, LGBTQ people, and any groups promoting liberal or anti-Catholic values – including the Freemasons, who were often openly critical of church doctrines. Under Franco's reign, Freemasons were subject to property seizures, kidnapping, and firing squads.

Aware of the doom that could befall the library if any Franco supporter came inside, the caretakers quietly locked the doors and opened for no one, lest the contents inside be pillaged. Years passed.

The library cautiously reopened in 1967, still bearing an ill reputation both for its freemason content and its writings that supported unions, workers, communism, and the free education of the working class.

Today, Barcelona bears a more tolerant disposition, and the books, having survived decades of peril, are ready to receive visitors again. "This is a well-preserved 19ᵗʰ-century library that has maintained its original design details," said Maribel Giner to *The Daily Beast* in 2020. "Stepping in here is like being transported to another era, and also an opportunity to explore a piece of Barcelona's history."

THE VATICAN APOSTOLIC ARCHIVES

VATICAN CITY

HOW TO FIND IT

Cortile del Belvedere, 00120 Città del Vaticano, Vatican City. +39 06 69883314; *archivioapostolico-vaticano.va*

While you can't visit the Vatican Apostolic Archives unless you are a permitted scholar, you may have an easier time getting into the Vatican Museums Library right next door. Founded in 1475, it houses journals and contemporary books that document the Vatican Museums' treasures.

Located just north of the Sistine Chapel, in heavily guarded rooms both above and below ground, the Vatican Apostolic Archives contains 85 km (53 miles) of documents spanning twelve centuries of the Holy Roman Empire's rule.

Officially, this is the Pope's private library. For most of its existence, no one was allowed to borrow or even view the books except members of the Holy See. Scholars of Christianity were not even permitted until 1881, when Pope Leo XIII, who had a reputation for embracing modernization, began to allow a select few inside.

Then, in 2011, Monsignor Sergio Pagano, prefect of the archives, decided to open the vaults to a carefully vetted publishing team. "A lot of hypotheses and all sorts of stories about the archive have been going around," he said in an interview. "We wanted to show the archive as it really is." The result of that 'peek' was a richly-imaged book called *Vatican Secret Archives*, which revealed to the rest of us what the sacred space had to offer.

Some notable items include documents from the 17th-century trial of Galileo Galilei, who was charged with heresy for asserting that the Earth revolved around the Sun. Another is the papal bull (official proclamation) of Pope Leo X, officially excommunicating Martin Luther from the Catholic Church. Yet another is the letter from King Henry VIII, requesting an annulment from his wife Catherine of Aragon, so he could marry Anne Boleyn (the Pope famously denied the request, resulting in Henry VIII's creation of the Anglican Church).

OPPOSITE The Vatican Apostolic Archive, formerly known as the Vatican Secret Archive, is considered the pope's private library, containing 1500 years of Roman Catholic history.

The physical structure of the library has expanded over the centuries under the guidance of various popes, and contains several floors, both above and below ground. They include a room of 16th-century frescos, whose solar observations formed the basis for the modern Gregorian calendar. A so-called diplomatic section holds official correspondence between the Roman Catholic Church and centuries of rulers of Europe. Beyond that are two above-ground sections known as the Noble Floor and the Chigi Rooms, as well as an underground structure known as The Bunker, which contains a dramatic 27 miles (43km) of shelves, designed to protect against fire, humidity, heat and other elemental stressors. Special documents are kept in private acclimatized rooms, located next to The Bunker.

Formerly known as The Vatican Secret Archives, in 2019, Pope Francis officially renamed the library The Vatican Apostolic Archives, to try and distance it from accusations of scandal and secrecy. The following March, he gave orders for the archive to be opened to the public. "The Church is not afraid of history," he said.

He sort of meant it. Documents less than 75 years old are still restricted from any public view. And the process for accessing the archives remains one of the most vigorous in the world. Authorizations are only provided to academic researchers who are empowered with a letter of recommendation from a reputable research institution. Once the letter is acquired, scholars must go through a short interview, conducted entirely in Italian. When authorized, individuals receive a specific letter inviting them to a subsection of the library. They take this letter to the Porta Sant'Anna, a side gate of the Vatican City, near the entrance to Saint Peter's, on an appointed day, and enter under the watch of the Swiss Guard. Researchers can access up to three pre-requested documents per day from the library, and access

"The process for accessing the archives remains one of the most vigorous in the world."

requests must be renewed every six months.

In a truly progressive move, in 2018, an innovative AI program known as In Codice Ratio began translating the 85 km (53 miles) of texts to make them searchable online. With so many well-preserved historic documents, so rarely studied by outside scholars, it is hard not to wonder if one contains a detail that could completely rewrite our perception of history.

LEFT The Sistine Hall is traditionally where rare public exhibitions are held. **BELOW** The Archive contains over 1 million texts, many of which are stored in an underground chamber known as 'The Bunker'.

THE LITTLE
FREE LIBRARY
AT THE
SOUTH POLE

GEOGRAPHIC SOUTH POLE, ANTARCTICA

HOW TO FIND IT

Geographic South Pole, Antarctic Plateau, Antarctica
nsf.gov/geo/opp/ support/southp.jsp

Typically, only specially employed people and the occasional journalist can visit either McMurdo Station or the interior of the ARO. However, Antarctic tour companies do organize excursions to the geographic South Pole where, during the summer, you may have a chance to peruse the bookshelves of Dr Schnell's cabinet next to the South Pole.

Antarctica is a land of extremes. Titanic rivers churn out waterfalls of powdered snow, mammoth ice flows sear sear the skyline with shades of alien blue, and the midnight ocean is so frigid, a dip for more than two minutes turns the average person's muscles to stone. For centuries, explorers have been captivated by these deadly landscapes, and hundreds have perished trying to mine the secrets locked away inside the thickest ice on Earth. Naturally, there are a few libraries.

As research stations began popping up on the outer edges of Antarctica in the 20th century, scientists flowed in. Many brought books with them. Like travelling to space, a journey to the South Pole commands a tidy packing list. There is only so much room on the boat for leisure material while attempting to stay alive in a place whose daily average temperature is -57°C (-7°F).

Distances between Antarctica's research-villages can be vast, but over the years many have amassed collections of books left behind by visiting scientists. The largest library, however, is at McMurdo Station. Established in 1956, McMurdo is designed to keep around 1000 people (a veritable megacity, by Antarctic

OPPOSITE The world's southernmost library poses for the camera on a rare sunny day.

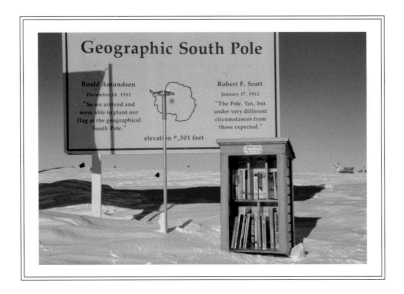

standard) sane and happy while living at the bottom of the Earth. Despite the icy tundra outside, step into McMurdo's community's library and you might forget where you are. Shelves of over 8000 books are organized into tidy aisles, flanked by cosy couches, and the rare green flashes of house plants. The collection contains a healthy number of scientific tomes, but also YA (young adult), fantasy, thriller and even some Shakespeare. There are also a few rather precious Antarctica histories, kept under lock and key.

However, despite the relatively professional aesthetics of the building, McMurdo's library has no official staff. It is run entirely on an honesty system, by scientists and other personnel who take a few hours away from their regular jobs each week to record checkouts, shelve returns, and generally keep the stacks organized. Patrons are asked to limit their selections to three books at a time, and to return their checkouts within three weeks. However, there are no late fees in Antarctica, and since researchers are often away on expeditions that can last months, everyone is rather

understanding if you return a book past its due date.

McMurdo is a necessary and beloved resource for the residents of the Antarctic. But there is another library, much smaller, and more hidden inside the opaque white winds of the southern continent: directly on top of the south pole.

Doctor Russell Schnell, a climate change research scientist and co-recipient of the 2007 Nobel Peace Prize, installed a Little Free Library on the geographic South Pole in 2020. The pint-sized wooden cabinet contains "books with photos of colorful trees, warm deserts, water, beaches, wheat fields, and animals and birds," Schnell said in a statement to Little Free Library in 2020, "Everything else is white for hundreds of miles in all directions."

The modest little library is trotted out next to the South Pole whenever weather allows – just in case anyone who might be passing by needs a book. However, when winter comes, the cabinet is brought inside the nearby Atmospheric Research Facility (ARO), where it is spared from the average -87°C (-125°F) temperatures and hurricane force winds.

BELOW The "Fridge Library" was first
created after public services shut down in
the wake of Christchurch's 2010 and 2011
catastrophic earthquakes.

THINK DIFFERENTLY BOOK EXCHANGE

HOW TO FIND IT

Kilmore and Barbadoes Streets, Christchurch, New Zealand
gapfiller.org.nz/project/think-differently-book-exchange/

The library got new owners in 2019 in the form of Pike Wholefoods, the supermarket across the street. The owners are committed to maintaining the little fridge's place in the neighbourhood.

CHRISTCHURCH, NEW ZEALAND

Between 2010 and 2011, a series of earthquakes hit New Zealand's South Island. Their magnitude ranged from 6.3 to 7.1. Some 10,000 homes were reduced to rubble or partially destroyed. Over 185 people perished. Power outages were widespread, and all non-essential services were shut down, including libraries.

Kiwis went into overdrive to repair what was broken, including librarians who saw an immediate need to get books into traumatized hands. So, in July 2011, five months after their second big quake, a giant catering refrigerator was set down across from Pike Wholefoods supermarket in Christchurch and filled with books.

The waterproof library at the corner of Kilmore and Barbadoes Streets was the brainchild of community arts initiative, Gapfiller, and local librarians. It was just meant to be temporary, a way to fill a suddenly vacated lot, and to provide a passable, if tiny, substitute for a real repository of books.

The library was officially dubbed the Think Differently Book Exchange. Neighbourhood residents were invited to come and stock the fridge with books that had altered their perspectives. The theme was local librarian Sarah Gallagher's idea. She didn't want a free library with just a random assortment of books. "Our world has been turned upside down...and I think we're all thinking differently

about life now," she said in 2011 on her personal website. "By asking people to bring along a book to share that inspired them to think differently…we thought perhaps it could help others think differently too."

Why a fridge? Coralie Winn, founder of Gap-filler, had initially planned for the site to be a cafe. But this idea had to be scrapped after she connected with Sarah Gallagher, who saw the need for a book exchange as a response to the city's library closures. The idea of a catering fridge – large, shelved, and waterproof – as a depository for the books quickly stuck.

When the library officially opened, over 100 people turned up with books in hand. "I was flat out for several hours registering books and explaining how the Book Exchange works," said Gallagher. "We had queues both at the deposit desk, and the fridge itself. It was tremendous and touching to see how excited people were about the project. Some people turned up with a carefully chosen book, a note inside explaining how it made them THINK DIFFERENTLY; others bought box loads."

The books are organized by genre, including fantasy, general fiction, non-fiction and kids. The sections are bookended by objects like milk bottles and mason jars.

Christchurch's traditional libraries have since reopened, but, more than ten years later, the fridge remains a post-quake icon.

BELOW Astronauts are permitted a small
number of books to take with them onto the
ISS. This has eventually led to a library
orbiting earth.

THE INTERNATIONAL SPACE STATION LIBRARY

OUTER SPACE

The astronauts who live on the International Space Station (ISS) have very few amenities to help pass the time – that is, when they're not conducting groundbreaking research or doing life-saving repairs.

Living on the Space Station means living with a sun that rises every 90 minutes, feeling like you have a constant head cold thanks to zero gravity, and sleeping buckled into a bed with seatbelts – lest your unconscious body floats away down the hall to wreak havoc. To top it off, astronauts are allotted a very finite amount of leisure items. Getting anything off Earth takes a tremendous amount of power, and so every inch of available volume in a rocket ship is meticulously accounted and planned for. Humans headed for a stay at the ISS are allotted a meagre 1.5kg (3.3lb) of material to put in their Personal Preference Kit (PPK).

Separate from each astronaut's PPK are crew care packages. These are drawn up by psychological support teams and include items considered to be essential for the wellbeing of the crewmembers, and often include movies, religious supplies, holiday decorations, favourite condiments and books.

When American astronaut Susan Helms was sent to the ISS in 2001, NASA granted her permission to bring a total of ten paperbacks. This is how paper copies of *Gone with the Wind*, *Vanity Fair* and *War and Peace* made it into space.

HOW TO FIND IT

The ISS moves around the sky in a low Earth orbit. Its current position can be found at esa.int. While you can't contact the astronauts on the ISS unless you are part of one of the organizing space programmes, you can sometimes find them chatting away on ham radio.

You can find past 'Story Time from Space' readings and educational videos at storytimefromspace.com

BELOW The ISS orbits the earth every 90 minutes.
OPPOSITE Astronaut Frank Rubio reads to earth's
children during Story Time from Space.

More than 20 years later, space tourists test-driving commercial interstellar space flights often bring books along with them to the ISS. When he took his first space flight in 2007, software engineer Charles Simonyi brought a copy of *Faust* along with Robert Heinlein's *The Moon is a Harsh Mistress.*

Today, the library on the ISS is well stocked with both books and movies. Sci-fi is a (perhaps surprisingly) popular genre in both departments, including such titles as *Alien Infection* by Darrell Bain, *The Moon's Shadow* by Catherine Asaro, and the films *2001: A Space Odyssey* and *Gravity.*

The library that has amassed on ISS has an extremely limited number of book titles (usually around 100). There is also no official librarian to keep them organized by Dewey decimal codes and ensure the astronauts are keeping their voices down. However, one thing it does have in common with your average terrestrial library is children's story time.

In 2014, the 'Story Time from Space' programme was launched by educator Patricia Tribe and astronaut Alvin Drew. The programme sends children's books to the ISS, whereupon an astronaut volunteers to make a video of themselves reading the book to the children of Earth – much like a librarian in an after-school club, just with far less gravity. The books are typically science and space themed, and the astronauts will often do an additional educational demonstration (designed by veteran astronaut Bjarni Tryggvason) to complement the concepts found in the book.

THE BANNED BOOK LIBRARY

ONLINE

There are hidden books, and then there are books that people are trying to hide.

Even in countries where freedom of speech is a prized value, there are books detailing ideas that some deem so incendiary, so threatening, so offensive that they are not merely restricted – they are banned.

Book bans have been a part of US history since before it declared independence from Britain. In the 1600s, John Morton's *New English Canaan* was banned for its outspoken critiques of Puritan customs. In 1873, US Congress passed the Act for the Suppression of Trade in, and Circulation of, Obscene Literature and Articles of Immoral Use – more commonly known as The Comstock Law. Under this act, everything from contraception education, photographs of boxing matches, and even the novels of DH Lawrence were outlawed, and literal tonnes of books containing 'immoral' material were destroyed.

If we observe the cycles of history, we can see, with some irony, that many books that start their careers with a 'banned' label find themselves being classified as 'required reading' some years later. Classics such as *The Color Purple, Lord of the Flies, To Kill a Mockingbird*, and *1984* have all been banned at one point – and then, a few decades later, found themselves on the syllabuses of high schools throughout the country.

Despite this repeated history, book bans have been on the rise since 2020. Between January and August of 2023, the American Library Association reported 1900 books were under censorship in various places across the county. School districts often vote to censor books to prevent age-inappropriate material from making its way into the hands of young children. But others argue this is

OPPOSITE A protester holds a sign at a school protest, encouraging administration to overturn a book ban.

"Between January and August of 2023,
the American Library Association reported
1900 books were under censorship in
various places across the county."

an overreach, a regression into a new version of the Comstock Law. "A year, a year and a half ago, we were told that these books didn't belong in school libraries, and if people wanted to read them, they could go to a public library," said Deborah Caldwell-Stone, the director of the American Library Association's Office for Intellectual Freedom, in a statement. "Now, we're seeing those same groups come to public libraries and come after the same books, essentially depriving everyone of the ability to make the choice to read them."

Most of today's banned books relate to the history of race segregation and slavery in the US or seek to educate young readers about LGBTQ people and culture. Some libraries have received bomb threats, lost funding, and had their librarians accused of paedophilia, simply for stocking these books.

In response, a number of public and private organizations have made an effort to make banned books more accessible than ever. This is a space where digital libraries truly shine. Although an e-reader or pdf robs a reader of the multi-sensory experience of holding a book in their hands, it is much more difficult to destroy or censor a digital book than a physical one.

In 2023, the Digital Public Library of America created a national resource to track all books currently banned across the country. "Our mission is to provide anyone who is in a library that has banned a book access to the digital version for free," says a statement on their website. The project is known as The Banned Book Club – a free, online library where anyone with an internet connection can access a book that has been banned. The books are available to be downloaded via a free app, known as The Palace Project. Anyone can visit them at www.thebanned-bookclub.info.

OPPOSITE Activists continue to organize to overturn book bans through legislation, and providing digital copies of banned books online.

BIBLIOGRAPHY

Arcadian Library
Warner, Marina. 'Inside the Secret Library Where East Meets West.'
The Times Literary Supplement, 2 November 2011, web.archive.
org/web/20120312110759/https://www.the-tls.co.uk/tls/public/arti-
cle812318.ece

Arús Public Library
Kliger, Isabelle. 'Barcelona's Best Hidden Gem May Be a Library for
the Working Class.' The Daily Beast, 11 August 2020, thedailybeast.
com/barcelonas-best-hidden-gem-may-be-a-library-for-the-working-
class

Banned Book Library
Alter, Alexandra and Elizabeth A. Harris. 'Book Bans Are Rising
Sharply in Public Libraries,' The New York Times, 21 September 2023,
nytimes.com/2023/09/21/books/book-ban-rise-libraries.html

Beach Library
'Life's a Beach for Readers in Bulgaria.' YouTube, uploaded by
euronews, 19 July 2013, youtube.com/watch?v=H7Pm60CbY0E

Bethnal Green Underground Library
Thompson, Kate. 'Bethnal Green's Underground Wartime Library.'
Historia, 24 February 2022, historiamag.com/bethnal-greens-under-
ground-wartime-library/

Bhadariya Temple Underground Library
Parihar, Rohit. 'Sadhu Brings a Nearly Dead Village in Rajasthan Back
to Life.' India Today, 27 December 1999, indiatoday.in/magazine/
offtrack/story/19991227-sadhu-brings-a-nearly-dead-village-in-ra-
jasthan-back-to-life-781282-1999-12-26

Bibliomotocarro
'Is This Italy's Smallest Library?' BBC, 29 January 2019, bbc.com/
culture/article/20190125-the-tiny-library-bringing-books-to-remote-
villages

Brautigan Library
Burbank, Megan. 'This Might Be the World's Only Library of
Unpublished Manuscripts: Vancouver's Brautigan Library Honors a
Northwest Literary Icon.' The Seattle Times, 10 April 2019, seattle-
times.com/entertainment/books/richard-brautigan-was-a-northwest-
literary-icon-in-a-tiny-library-in-vancouver-his-legacy-lives-on/

Future Library
Anne Beate. Personal interview. 6 March 2023.

Home Library of Bruno Shröder
Kleinhubbert, Guido. 'The Old Man's Secret.' Der Spiegel, 20 January
2023, spiegel.de/wissenschaft/mettingen-wohin-mit-der-wahrschein-
lich-groessten-privatbibliothek-deutschlands-a-7d5dcdfc-15bb-4a83-
a5f5-e118abd87344

Horse Library
Malcolm Clark. Personal interview. 18 December 2023.

KIDS Corner Library
McMullen, Colin. 'The Corner Libraries.' 10 January 2013, emceecm.
com/libraries/

Kurkku Fields Underground Library
'Library in the Earth.' Hiroshi Nakamura & NAP, n.d, https://www.
nakam.info/en/works/library-in-the-earth/

Les Archives Nationales
Wolff-Fineout, Noa. 'Paris' Dusty Diary: A Peek Inside the City's
Most Secret Library.' Messy Nessy, 10 October 2019, messynessychic.
com/2017/06/23/paris-dusty-diary-a-peek-inside-the-citys-most-
secret-library/

The Libraries of Chinguetti
Longari, Marco and Ruby Mellen. 'Mauritania's Ancient Libraries
Could Be Lost to the Expanding Desert.' The Washington Post, 20
March 2023, washingtonpost.com/world/interactive/2023/maurita-
nia-libraries-desert/

Little Free Library in a Cottonwood Tree
Strickland, Cara. 'The Most Magical 'Little Free Library' Is Built
Right Into a Tree Stump.' Atlas Obscura, 18 January 2019, https://
www.atlasobscura.com/places/little-free-library-in-a-110-year-old-
tree-stump

Little Free Library at the South Pole
Aldrich, Margret. 'This Little Free Library at the South Pole Is the
First in Antarctica,' 10 December 2020, Little Free Library, https://
littlefreelibrary.org/2020/12/this-little-free-library-at-the-south-pole-
is-the-first-in-antarctica/

Levinsky Garden Library
'The Garden Library for Refugees and Migrant Workers / Yoav Meiri
Architects.' ArchDaily, 20 February 2011, archdaily.com/112495/
the-garden-library-for-refugees-and-migrant-workers-yoav-meiri-
architects

Lonely Library
'Seashore Library / Vector Architects.' ArchDaily, 2 June 2015, arch-daily.com/638390/seashore-library-vector-architects

Mogao Grottoes
Stein, Marc Aurel. Ruins of Desert Cathay: Personal Narrative of Explorations in Central Asia and Westernmost China. NII 'Digital Silk Road' / Toyo Bunko. doi:10.20676/00000213.

People's Library of Occupy Wall Street
Norton, Daniel; Henk, Mandy; Fagin, Betsy; Taylor, Jaime; Loeb, Zachary. 'Occupy Wall Street Librarians Speak Out.' Progressive Librarian. Issue 38/39, 2012, pp. 7–8
LeVine, Mark. 'The People's Library and the Future of OWS.' Al Jazeera, 17 November 2011, aljazeera.com/opinions/2011/11/17/the-peoples-library-and-the-future-of-ows
'ALA Alarmed at Seizure of Occupy Wall Street Library, Loss of Irreplaceable Material.' American Library Association, 17 November 2011, ala.org/news/press-releases/2011/11/ala-alarmed-seizure-occu-py-wall-street-library-loss-irreplaceable-material

Prison Library Project
Perez, Sergio. Personal interview. 11 December 2023.

Reading Club 2000
Henley, Jon. 'The Library with No Rules.' The Guardian, 23 September 2012, theguardian.com/books/shortcuts/2012/sep/23/the-library-with-no-rules

Sakya Monastery Library
Lang, Zhao 'Tibet's Sakya Monastery Completed Digitized Leaf-by-Leaf Scanning of 20% of Ancient Books.' China Tibet Magazine, 28 February 2022, http://m.tibet.cn/cn/book/202202/t20220228_7153903.html

St Catherine's Monastery
Father Justin of Sinai. 'St. Catherine's Monastery, Its Library, and Its Palimpsests.' Sinai Palimpsests Project. n.d. http://sinaipalimpsests.org/st-catherine%E2%80%99s-monastery-its-library-and-its-palimp-sests/index.html

Stony Island Arts Bank
Budds, Diana. 'The Stony Island Arts Bank Brings 'Redemptive Architecture' To Chicago's South Side.' Fast Company, 6 October 2015, fastcompany.com/3051918/the-stony-island-arts-bank-brings-redemptive-architecture-to-chicagos-south-side

Street Books
Johnson, Kirk. 'Homeless Outreach in Volumes: Books by Bike for 'Outside' People in Oregon.' The New York Times, 9 October 2014, nytimes.com/2014/10/10/us/homeless-outreach-in-volumes-books-by-bike-for-outside-people-in-oregon.html

Strength of Words
'Game Changer: The Garbage Collector Who Spreads Books' You-Tube, uploaded by CGTN America, 10 February 2017, youtube.com/watch?v=mojbzxNBSeM

Timbuktu Manuscripts
Tattersall, Nick. 'Libraries in the Sand Reveal Africa's Academic Past.' Reuters, 9 August 2007, reuters.com/article/idUSL10685745/

Traveler Restaurant
Gordon, Ilana. 'At the Traveler Restaurant, It's Totally Okay to Read While You Eat.' The Takeout, 9 November 2020, https://thetakeout.com/at-the-traveler-restaurant-read-books-while-you-eat-1845534938

Think Differently Book Exchange
Gallagher, Sarah. 'Gap Filler Think Differently Book Exchange,' 12 May 2011, https://sarahlibrarina.tumblr.com/gapfiller

Weapon of Mass Instruction
' 7UP® I Feels Good To Be You™ I RAUL - A WEAPON OF MASS INSTRUCTION.' YouTube, uploaded by My 7UP, 11 May 2015, youtube.com/watch?v=kwMc0pHkQ5s

Hidden Libraries
October 2024
Published by Lonely Planet Global Limited
CRN 554153
www.lonelyplanet.com
10 9 8 7 6 5 4 3 2 1

Printed in Malaysia
ISBN 978 1837582723 3
© Lonely Planet 2024
© photographers as indicated 2024

Publishing Director Piers Pickard
Publisher Becca Hunt
Author Diana Helmuth
Designer Emily Dubin
Editors Joanna Cooke; Alison Throckmorten
Print Production Nigel Longuet

STAY IN TOUCH lonelyplanet.com/contact

Lonely Planet Global Limited
Digital Depot, Roe Lane (off Thomas St),
Digital Hub, Dublin 8,
D08 TCV4
Ireland

Front cover photos © Su Shengliang; © BC architects & studies;
© Yuka Yanazume
Back cover photo © Pavel Adashkevich | Alamy Stock Photo
Book icon © Kurdanfell | Shutterstock
Endsheet pattern © Andy Magee | Shutterstock

Paper in this book is certified against the
Forest Stewardship Council™ standards.
FSC™ promotes environmentally responsible,
socially beneficial and economically viable
management of the world's forests.